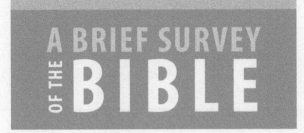

A BRIEF SURVEY
OF THE BIBLE

A BRIEF SURVEY OF THE BIBLE

Discovering the Big Picture of God's Story from Genesis to Revelation

STUDY GUIDE   **14 SESSIONS**

JOHN WALTON & MARK STRAUSS

ZONDERVAN®

ZONDERVAN

A Brief Survey of the Bible Study Guide
Copyright © 2015 by Zondervan

This title is also available as a Zondervan ebook. Visit www.zondervan.com/ebooks.

Requests for information should be addressed to:

Zondervan, 3900 *Sparks Dr. SE, Grand Rapids, Michigan* 49546

ISBN 978-0-310-89489-6

Sources used for the "Did You Know?" and "Overview" sections:

Zondervan Handbook to the Bible, © 1999 Pat and David Alexander.

Zondervan NIV Study Bible, Copyright © 1985, 1995, 2002, 2008, 2011 by The Zondervan Corporation.

You Are Here in the Bible, Copyright © 2001, 2002, 2003 by Ted Cooper Jr.

Cover design: *John Hamilton Design*
Cover photography: *iStockphoto.com*
Interior design: *Denise Froehlich*

First Printing October 2015 / Printed in the United States of America

Contents

How to Use This Guide

A Brief Survey of the Bible is designed to be experienced in a group setting such as a Bible study, Sunday school class, or any small group gathering. In addition to bringing a Bible to group discussions, you will want to have your own study guide, which includes notes for video segments, directions for activities and discussion questions, and personal studies and reading plans to deepen learning between sessions. Each group should also have one copy of the *A Brief Survey of the Bible* video for group viewing.

Each session begins with an opening question to get the group comfortable interacting with each other. You will then watch the video with John Walton (for the Old Testament) or Mark Strauss (for the New Testament) and jump into some directed small group discussion. Note that while many questions have been provided for your small group, you shouldn't feel that you have to cover them all. The facilitator will focus on the ones that resonate most with your group and guide the discussion from there. In addition, to ensure everyone has enough time to participate in discussions, it is recommended that you break up large groups into smaller groups of four to six people.

The final activity in each session is called "Living the Word." In this section, your group will engage in some practical exercises to help you move the message of the study from the head to the heart. Think of this time as an answer to the question, "How do I apply what we've just covered in the Bible to my life?" These exercises will be what you make of them. If you choose to just go through the motions, or if you abstain from participating, there is a lesser chance you'll find what you're looking for in this survey of the Bible. But if you stay open and take this step, you will discover what so many others have found to be true: faith comes alive when you take risks for God!

The bulk of the Bible reading you will do during the course of this study will take place in between times with your group. For this reason, each session includes an "On Your Own" section that provides (1) a brief overview of the books of the Bible you will be studying, (2) a five-day reading plan with selected stories and passages from Scripture, and (3) a few reflection questions based on the Scripture you read to help you solidify the key points in your mind.

The most important part of the between-sessions work is the Bible reading, as you will want to be familiar with the material before the next session begins. For this reason, if you get behind, try to read some extra pages on another day until you are caught up. If you get *way* behind, consider setting aside a larger block of time — such as a Sunday afternoon — to go through the readings. At first this may seem more like a chore than a spiritual experience, but you will be surprised by the insights you glean if you follow this course.

May God bless you as you seek to learn more about his character, his nature, his work, and his presence in your life through this study of his Word.

Note: If you are a facilitator, there are additional instructions and resources in the back of the book for leading the group discussion times.

An Introduction to

A Brief Survey of the Bible

And beginning with Moses and all the Prophets, he explained to them what was said in all the Scriptures concerning himself.

LUKE 24:27

WELCOME

Welcome to session 1 of *A Brief Survey of the Bible*. If this is your first time together as a group, take a moment to introduce yourselves to each other. Then go around the group and answer the following questions:

• What three adjectives best describe your attitude toward reading the Bible?

• What is your primary reason for wanting to do a survey of the Bible?

WATCH THE VIDEO

Play the video teaching segment for session 1. As you watch, use the following outline to record any thoughts or concepts that stand out to you.

Notes

The Old Testament is God's story — God's revelation of himself. If we are going to serve him, know him, love him, we have to know his story.

The whole idea of the Bible is to help us understand God's big plan for things. In the beginning God created a place for us, and he would dwell there with us so we could be in relationship with him. Sin disrupted that relationship — we no longer had access to God's presence.

God initiated the covenant with Abraham. By making a relationship with Abraham, God was reestablishing his presence among people.

At the end of the kingdom period, everything was in jeopardy and God was about to pick up and leave. Yet God had already talked about Immanuel — God with us.

God is a God of grace, and he launched a rescue plan. This plan involved a man and a nation. God made a covenant with Abraham, and all nations would be blessed through him. It was through the line of Abraham that God would bring a Savior.

The Old Testament gives us the stories that help us understand what kind of God he is. Only when we understand God's character can we appreciate his presence in us and seek after a relationship that will please him, honor him, and allow us to serve in relationship with him.

The central theme of the Old Testament is promise. The central theme of the New Testament is fulfillment of that promise in the life, death, and resurrection of Jesus the Messiah.

Jesus is the center point of salvation history. Jesus is the one prophesied in the Old Testament. The story in Luke 24 summarizes the whole message of the Bible: through Jesus, God has acted to bring his people back into a right relationship with him.

GROUP DISCUSSION

Take a few minutes with your group members to discuss what you just watched and explore these concepts in Scripture.

1. After watching the video, what is your primary motivation for reading the Bible?

2. What challenges and benefits do you anticipate as you participate in this study?

3. What most excites you about the prospect of doing this survey of the Bible?

4. As you do this study, what do you expect to discover in terms of practical living, spiritual growth, knowledge of history, or other areas?

5. What do you hope to learn about God by reading his story?

6. How can knowing God's story build your relationship with him?

7. God's love story is one of promises and fulfillment, of pursuit and restoration. How do these qualities of God, and his passion for his people, encourage you to trust him?

LIVING THE WORD

For this activity, each group member will need a blank piece of paper, a pen, and an envelope.

In this session, you have seen that the Bible is God's love story — his revelation of himself to his people in order to establish a relationship with us. This story comes to fruition through Jesus, who was God fulfilling his promise to dwell with us and bless us. On the blank piece of paper, describe the relationship you have with God right now. Then describe the ways in which you would like your relationship with God to grow during the course of this study. Date and sign your paper and seal it in the envelope. Keep it in your Bible as a reminder of your desire to grow closer to God. At the end of the study, you will read your description and write a new one based on any areas of spiritual growth that you have experienced.

CLOSING PRAYER

Use the following prayer to close out your group time, or feel free to say one of your own.

> God, you've invited each of us here to embark on this study of your Word. While we understand the parameters of this journey and may have some idea where it will lead, we also know unanticipated twists and turns await us. Ultimately, we believe there are significant truths you want to teach us about you, the world, and ourselves. As each of us prays our silent decision to you, we ask that you give us the strength to respond to your desires more strongly than to our own. Hear us as we each pray. In your Son's name, amen.

On Your Own
Between-Sessions
Personal Study

This week, you listened to an opening introduction from John Walton and Mark Strauss about how the Bible is the story of God's revelation of himself and about his pursuit of a loving relationship with his creation. In the next session, you will be discussing key stories and principles from the books of Genesis and Exodus. Use the following between-sessions material to give you some background on these books and guide your reading for the week.

OVERVIEW

The following is a brief overview of the books you and your group will cover during next week's session. Take a moment to review this information, and at the end of the section note any questions you want to discuss with your group.

Genesis

Genesis is the book of beginnings and sets the stage for everything that follows in the Bible. It establishes God as the creator of all that is — in heaven, on earth, and beyond. Genesis focuses on the essential relationship of humanity, the one that exists between God and the people he created, and introduces us to the way God makes covenants with them. In Genesis we witness Satan entice Adam and Eve to disobey God, which establishes the central conflict of human history. The remainder of the Bible is the story of how God resolves that loss of relationship. Historically, Jews and Christians have held that Moses was the author of the first five books of the Bible, writing to God's chosen people, the Israelites, around 1446 to 1406 BC.

Exodus

The word *Exodus* means "exit" or "departure," and the book describes the Israelite people's journey from slavery in Egypt to the threshold of the Promised Land in Canaan. Yet Exodus is not only the story of Israel's departure from the land of Egypt but also the story of Israel's departure from the lifestyle of Egypt. It is not merely a journey of time and distance but also a journey of the heart, as a holy God prepares his chosen people to live the life he offers in the land he has provided. In Exodus he reveals his name, his attributes, his redemption, his Law, and how he is to be worshiped, and then he invites his people into relationship with him.

READING

Each day this week, read the passages of Scripture indicated below. If it is helpful, use this chart to help you record your reading progress. Establish a reading schedule that works best for you — and then stick with it. Try to make it a habit to pray before you begin reading each day, asking God to use his Word to instruct and guide you.

Day	Passage	☑
1	Genesis 1 – 3; 5 – 11	☐
2	Genesis 12; 15 – 16; 18 – 19; 21:1 – 7; 25:19 – 34; 27	☐
3	Genesis 37; 39 – 46; 50	☐
4	Exodus 1; 3 – 5; 7 – 11; 13:17 – 14:31	☐
5	Exodus 19 – 20; 25:1 – 9; 26 – 32; 39:32 – 40:38	☐

STUDY QUESTIONS

1. What are some of the highlights — knowledge gained, puzzling questions, moments of insight — you experienced during your reading this week?

2. How would you describe God's response to his creation of Adam and Eve (see Genesis 1:27 – 31; 2:4 – 8, 15 – 25)? How did Adam and Eve's disobedience change their relationship with God (see Genesis 3)?

3. Why did the people want to build the tower of Babel (see Genesis 11:1 – 9)? How did God feel about their efforts?

4. What did God ask Abraham to do in Genesis 12:1? What promise did God make to Abraham? How did God keep this promise (see Genesis 21:1 – 7)?

5. What obstacles did God overcome in Joseph's life? What was Joseph's response to God's presence in his life? How would you describe Joseph's relationship with God?

6. What was God trying to show Moses and the Egyptians through both the miraculous signs he performed and the plagues (see Exodus 7:5 and 14:4)?

7. What message does God give Moses in Exodus 19:4 – 6? How does God show his presence among the Israelites while they are in the desert?

8. Briefly list the Ten Commandments (see Exodus 20). What was God's purpose in giving his people these laws (see verse 20)? Why did God instruct the Israelites to build the tabernacle (see Exodus 25:8)?

Use the space below to write down any key points or questions you want to bring to the next group meeting.

A Brief Survey of
Genesis – Exodus

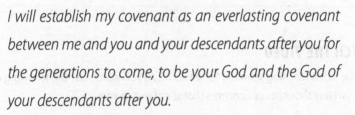

*I will establish my covenant as an everlasting covenant
between me and you and your descendants after you for
the generations to come, to be your God and the God of
your descendants after you.*

GENESIS 17:7

WELCOME

Welcome to session 2 of *A Brief Survey of the Bible*. Take a few minutes to go around the group and invite everyone to answer the following questions:

- What situations help you get to know another person better?
- Name two blessings that you have received. Why do you consider these to be blessings?

READING FOLLOW-UP

1. What challenges did you face in getting your reading done? What was the most effective thing you did to meet those challenges?

2. As you read the Bible this week, what particular thoughts and/or events stood out to you or surprised you? Why?

3. What questions came up during your reading for which you'd like to find answers?

WATCH THE VIDEO

Play the video teaching segment for session 2. As you watch, use the following outline to record any thoughts or concepts that stand out to you.

Notes

Genesis is not just the story of how this world we live in began but also how God's presence first began in it. God is creating a place that he is going to come to and dwell in.

Humanity's greatest loss in the garden of Eden was the loss of God's presence.

Genesis 1 – 11 reveals how sin progressed in the world and how the people lost and distorted the true knowledge of God.

Genesis 12 – 50 describes how God initiated a plan to reveal himself anew to these people who had lost the knowledge of him. God used the means of a covenant and sought out a man named Abraham to bring blessing to the whole world.

God can always snatch blessing from the throes of disaster, from the pits of sinfulness and evil. By revealing himself, God was working to reestablish his presence with humankind.

All the Law is premised on the concept that God is holy and we are also to be holy.

The tabernacle was the means by which God intended to reestablish his presence. It was his foothold in this world — built by God's initiative to show the people how he was to be treated. The Law instructed the people on how to *manage* God's presence in their midst.

Exodus 40:34 points out that God's presence among the people was in a limited way, in a restricted place, and with restricted access.

GROUP DISCUSSION

Take a few minutes with your group members to discuss what you just watched and explore these concepts in Scripture.

1. As you watched the video, which particular points stood out to you? Which aspect of the video most enhanced your understanding of what you read this past week?

2. Adam and Eve's sin resulted in the loss of God's presence in their lives. What were the consequences of that loss? How has it affected us to this day?

3. God took the initiative to reveal himself to his people by making a covenant with Abraham. What are some ways God reveals himself to people today? How can this affect our relationship with him?

4. Like Joseph, sometimes we can experience obstacles in our lives that make it difficult to see God's purpose. What can you learn from Joseph about handling situations in which God seems distant? How does this change your perspective of obstacles you may encounter?

5. The Law that God gave to Moses helped the people understand that the Lord was holy and wanted his people to be holy. What does it mean to be *holy*? What does living a holy life look like today?

6. What picture of God are you developing through your reading so far? What are some of God's characteristics and attributes that you have observed? How have you seen him demonstrate those to his chosen people?

7. What did God reveal through the tabernacle about his commitment to be with his people? How does God's presence in our lives change the way we live?

8. What would you identify as the key themes of this portion of Scripture? What impact will what you've just studied make on your life today?

LIVING THE WORD

For this activity, everyone will need a quarter, two light-colored ¾-inch round labels, and a permanent marker.

Team up with another person (or two) in your group and briefly share three obstacles you are currently facing (for example, an issue with your job, a relationship, or a health concern). Then share three ways God has blessed you and whether there were any times when God turned an obstacle into a blessing. After you have discussed these, write on your labels one blessing from God and one obstacle, and then apply the labels to the two sides of the quarter. Keep this coin in your pocket or in a visible place to remind you that God reveals his presence to us through both blessings and obstacles, so we need to look for him in every situation. Also look for ways during the coming week to encourage those who are facing a Joseph-like situation.

CLOSING PRAYER

Use the following prayer to close out your group time, or feel free to say one of your own.

> *Thank you, God, that you take the initiative to establish a relationship with us. Help us to recognize your presence and purpose in our lives, through both the blessings and obstacles we experience. May we, through your power, grow closer to you and become your holy people.*

Did You Know?

- The book of Genesis establishes four great principles that are crucial to our understanding of God's Word: (1) God brings order out of chaos by making distinctions and setting limits; (2) humans were created in the image and likeness of God, but after the fall we retained the image but not the likeness; (3) life involves choices and choices have consequences; and (4) Satan's strategy is to humanize God (make us doubt the Word), minimize sin (make us deny the Word), and deify man (make us replace the Word).

- The ancient Egyptians revered and worshiped many gods, including snakes. When God had Moses' staff miraculously become a snake and swallow up the magicians' snakes (see Exodus 7:8 – 13), he was demonstrating his power over Pharaoh and Egypt's gods. Furthermore, the plagues God sent to the Egyptians directly confronted and rebuked their worship of other gods. The Nile River, which turned to blood, was linked to the god Hapi. Frogs were linked to the goddess Heqt. The cows that died during the live-stock plague were linked to Hathor, the cow-god; Khnum, the ram-god; and the Egyptian bull-gods Apis and Mnevis. God wanted the ancient Egyptians

---

to realize that he alone was God Almighty, *Yahweh*, the "I AM WHO I AM" (Exodus 3:14). (*NIV Study Bible*)

- God instructed Moses to have the people build a tabernacle so that God could have a visible place to live among his people. The building and furnishing of the tabernacle used the people's skills in spinning, weaving, and dying fibers; embroidery; rounding, polishing, and engraving precious and semi-precious stones; and gold and silver work. They gladly committed their work and wealth to "God's tent," and when it was completed, the visible symbols of God's presence — his cloud by day and the fire by night — rested on the tabernacle and filled it with the light of his glory. For the next three hundred years, until Solomon built the temple in Jerusalem, the tabernacle was the focus of the nation's worship. (*Zondervan Handbook to the Bible*)

On Your Own
Between-Sessions Personal Study

This week, you explored God's story in the books of Genesis and Exodus. In the next session, you will be discussing key stories and principles from the books of Leviticus – Deuteronomy. Use the following between-sessions material to give you some background on these books and guide your reading for the week.

OVERVIEW

The following is a brief overview of the books you and your group will cover during next week's session. Take a moment to review this information, and at the end of the section note any questions you want to discuss with your group.

Leviticus

Leviticus is essentially the rulebook for Israel's priests (the "Levites"). All the laws spring from God's covenant with his chosen people. The Hebrews had grown up in slavery, so these laws were part of the process God used to mold them into the people they needed to be before they entered into the Promised Land. These laws were about relationships — those they were to have with one another and the one they were to have with their God. As you read, notice the unchanging character of God and our human need for forgiveness and a restored relationship with him. Leviticus helps us understand why we need to be holy and why it was necessary for Jesus to stand in our place and die for our sins.

Numbers

The English name of the book comes from the census lists found in chapters 1 and 26, but the Hebrew name of the book, meaning "in the desert," is more descriptive of what it is about. As the Israelites approached the Promised Land of Canaan, moving from Mount Sinai to the plains of Moab, they had to choose whether or not to trust their God. As you read, notice what happens when they focus on their circumstances and feelings rather than on what God has promised to do for them. Also note how after denying God's character and promises, they must face his judgment—thirty-eight more years in the wilderness.

Deuteronomy

Deuteronomy is the last of the five "Books of Moses," also known as the Torah or Pentateuch, delivered by Moses before transferring leadership of the people to Joshua. Within its pages, you'll experience your first dose of extended repetition in the Bible. While this can make for tedious reading, the repetition can help you order biblical events more firmly in your mind. Deuteronomy is important because it greatly influenced Judah and Israel's prophets, who in turn influenced key New Testament figures. As you read, notice the emphasis on worshiping God and God alone. Also note how often Moses mentions that God will fulfill his promise to Abraham and give the Israelites the Promised Land, and pay attention to the predictions God instructs Moses to give concerning Israel. Imagine what it would have been like to be camped on the east side of the Jordan River, poised to enter Canaan, and to hear these words from Moses. Finally, notice the choice Joshua and Moses urged the people to make so God would bless them with a full, productive, and meaningful life (see Deuteronomy 30:19–20; 32:44–47).

READING

Each day this week, read the passages of Scripture indicated below. If it is helpful, use this chart to help you record your reading progress. Establish a reading schedule that works best for you—and then stick with it. Try to make it a habit to pray before you begin reading each day, asking God to use his Word to instruct and guide you. If you find you are behind in your reading, set aside extra time this week to catch up.

Day	Passage	☑
1	Leviticus 1 – 5; 10 – 11; 13; 16	☐
2	Leviticus 19 – 23; 25; Numbers 1; 6	☐
3	Numbers 10 – 14; 16; 20 – 21	☐
4	Numbers 22 – 24; 27:12 – 23; Deuteronomy 1 – 3	☐
5	Deuteronomy 4 – 6; 10; 12 – 13; 17	☐

STUDY QUESTIONS

1. What are some of the highlights — knowledge gained, puzzling questions, moments of insight — you experienced during your reading this week?

2. Leviticus 10:8 – 11 gives us a glimpse of God's requirements for his people to be holy — especially the priests who served in the tabernacle. What does God's standard of holiness tell us about his character?

3. God's presence with the Israelites was physically manifested through signs such as the pillar of fire/cloud and the resources he provided to his people. In Numbers 11 – 13, how did the people respond to God's provision of food, Moses' leadership, and the conquest of the Promised Land? How do these reactions show us that the generation who had left Egypt had failed in their relationship with God?

4. Numbers 22 – 24 reveals God bringing a new blessing to his people — to the generation who *would* enter the Promised Land. What did Balak ask Balaam to do to the Israelites? How did God use Balaam to bless his people? Summarize the blessings Balaam pronounced over Israel (see especially 23:21 – 24; 24:3 – 9).

5. God named Joshua to succeed Moses and lead the new generation into the Promised Land (see Numbers 27:12 – 22). Why was Moses not allowed to enter the land? What words of encouragement did Moses give to Joshua when he finally handed the mantle of leadership to him (see Deuteronomy 31:1 – 8)?

6. In Deuteronomy 1:19 – 46, Moses provided the Israelites with a look back at their rebellious history as they traveled from Egypt to the Promised Land. What was different about Caleb and Joshua? How did God describe them? What does this tell you about what pleases God?

7. The Law was available to every person (see Deuteronomy 26:16 – 27:8), and God's requirements were clear. What blessings did God offer for the people's obedience? What consequences did he decree for their disobedience (see Deuteronomy 28)?

8. In spite of the Israelites' repeated disobedience, God renewed his covenant with them. What was required of the people to keep their part of the covenant (see Deuteronomy 29:12 – 13; 30:11 – 20)? How did Moses prepare the people to enter into the Promised Land and not fail a second time?

Use the space below to write down any key points or questions you want to bring to the next group meeting.

A Brief Survey of
Leviticus – Deuteronomy

Be holy because I, the LORD your God, am holy.

LEVITICUS 19:2

WELCOME

Welcome to session 3 of *A Brief Survey of the Bible*. Take a few minutes to go around the group and invite everyone to answer the following questions:

- In what ways does the United States Constitution and the Bill of Rights define our character as a nation?
- What do your household rules say about the character and attitudes you want your family members to display?

READING FOLLOW-UP

1. What challenges did you face in getting your reading done? What was the most effective thing you did to meet those challenges?

2. As you read the Bible this week, what particular thoughts and/or events stood out to you or surprised you? Why?

3. What questions came up during your reading for which you'd like to find answers?

WATCH THE VIDEO

Play the video teaching segment for session 3. As you watch, use the following outline to record any thoughts or concepts that stand out to you.

Notes

God's holiness is not just one characteristic alongside the others. Rather, his holiness is the result of all the other attributes. Everything that God is, together, makes him holy.

God calls us to separate ourselves from those around us. Holiness is about imitating God.

Once God took up residence among his people, it was important for them to respond to him properly. Having God's presence was a great benefit for the Israelites, but they had to handle his holiness properly, for there was danger there.

The sacrifices described in the early chapters of Leviticus were meant to help the people work with God's presence. Human sin had a way of desecrating and dirtying God's presence, and the sacrifices were needed to keep God's presence in its proper condition.

Today, as Christians, we have God's presence in us, individually and corporately. We need to be just as concerned about caring for God's presence as the Israelites were instructed to be in Leviticus.

Numbers has two basic aspects to it. The first is the rebellion of the people. The second has to do with transition — the transition from the generation who failed to the generation who was prepared to take up the mantle and gain the promises of God in the land.

Deuteronomy is God's "charter" — the renewal of God's covenant with this new generation.

The Ten Commandments are the centerpiece of God's revelation of himself through the Law. They tell us as much about God as they tell us about what God expects from us.

GROUP DISCUSSION

Take a few minutes with your group members to discuss what you just watched and explore these concepts in Scripture.

1. As you watched the video, which particular points stood out to you? Which aspect of the video most enhanced your understanding of what you read this past week?

2. How did God enable the people of the Old Testament to be holy? Why should we be concerned about personal and corporate holiness today?

3. How does sin affect our relationship with God? What choices do we have in dealing with sin?

4. Despite all that God had done for them, the Israelites repeatedly disobeyed, complained, and turned away from him. What kinds of temptations drew the Israelites away from God? How different are these from our temptations and complaints?

5. What was it about Joshua that pleased God? How can we be more like him in our relationship with God? What would this look like for us today?

6. What do we learn about God's commitment to a right relationship with us through his covenant promises? What is our part in the relationship?

7. What do the Ten Commandments tell us about God? Why should we take God's Law seriously?

8. Moses and Joshua were responsible for presenting God's Law to the people, guiding them in obedience to the Law, and correcting them in their disobedience as God directed. How do we exert this same influence today? What impact can we have on others?

LIVING THE WORD

For this activity, each group member will need a copy of the Ten Commandments printed on one side of a piece of card stock.

—∞—

Praying Scripture can have a powerful effect in your life. Take a few moments to pray through the Ten Commandments, personalizing each one with the pronoun "I." On the back of the card, write down a specific situation in which you need God's help to be holy and obedient to him. Share with another person in your group what you have written, and then pray for one another. Contact that person during the week so you can encourage each other in your efforts and hold each other accountable to personal holiness.

CLOSING PRAYER

Use the following prayer to close out your group time, or feel free to say one of your own.

Lord Jesus, it is only by your power and sacrifice for our sins that we can be made holy. Thank you for taking the initiative to restore our relationship with God. Thank you for your Word that helps us know you and follow your example of holiness. We ask for the wisdom to respect your presence in our lives and that you would cleanse us from sin. Amen.

Did You Know?

- The holiness of God is the dominant theme of Leviticus. In fact, the word *holy* appears more times in Leviticus than in any other book of the Bible. In just nine chapters of the book, God states, "I am the LORD" forty-seven times. (*NIV Study Bible*, note for Leviticus 18:2)

- Although the Old Testament requirements for cleanliness and perfection may offend modern readers, it is important to remember that God is perfect and we are not. Just as Israel was required to sacrifice perfect animals in order to maintain their relationship with a holy God, we also need a perfect substitute for our sins. Jesus provided that substitute when he sacrificed himself for us on the cross.

- The same Hebrew word used for an international treaty is also used for a covenant between God and his people. The Sinai covenant, the most important Old Testament covenant, was the key step in Israel's becoming a nation. It followed the covenant God made with Noah (see Genesis 9) and the two covenants God made with Abraham (see Genesis 15 and 17). At Sinai, God not only gave his Law to Israel but also called them to be holy and to give him exclusive allegiance. He called them as a nation into a new relationship with him. (*Zondervan Handbook to the Bible*)

On Your Own
Between-Sessions
Personal Study

This week, you explored God's story in the books from Leviticus – Deuteronomy. In the next session, you will be discussing key stories and principles from the books of Joshua – 1 Samuel. Use the following between-sessions material to give you some background on these books and guide your reading for the week.

OVERVIEW

The following is a brief overview of the books you and your group will cover during next week's session. Take a moment to review this information, and at the end of the section note any questions you want to discuss with your group.

Joshua

After many years of slavery in Egypt and forty years of wandering in the wilderness, God finally brought the Israelites into Canaan and began to fulfill the promises he made to the patriarchs. Take note of Joshua's faithfulness to God as he leads Israel in conquering the Canaanites, which is one of the high points of Israel's history. Joshua's faithful leadership brings great reward to the nation, but even so, Israel is not entirely faithful in obeying God's commands. The book was written by an unknown author around 1390 BC, though some sections may derive from Joshua himself.

Judges

The title of this book refers to the leaders (Hebrew *shophet*) God raised at certain times to rid the Israelites of foreign invaders. The invaders came into the land as a result of the people's disobedience to God and rejection of his kingship — a theme that occurs early in the book and repeats throughout. Note the strengths and weaknesses of the various judges — including Deborah, Gideon, and Samson — whom God sent to assist Israel. Consider also the cycle that begins during this period: Israel breaks its covenant with God; God sends oppressors to punish them; they cry out for help; he delivers them; and then they disobey again. Judges was written by an unknown author around 1000 BC, though some sections may have been penned by the prophet Samuel.

Ruth

The book of Ruth is set during the time of the judges, which explains its placement in our modern Bibles (in the Hebrew Bible it appears after the Song of Solomon or Song of Songs). In many ways the book, which reads like a short story, portrays the promise of a life far beyond our expectations. As you read, take note of the themes of faithful love and redemption that prevail as events unfold for an Israelite family. Ruth was penned by an unknown author sometime after David became king of Israel in about 1010 BC.

1 Samuel

The book of 1 Samuel is named after the prophet and judge whom God used to establish the monarchy in Israel. The events in the book take place during a time of national political, social, and spiritual turmoil. Observe how the people refuse to listen to God and make the rough transition from the time of the judges to the reign of Saul, whom God calls Samuel to anoint as Israel's first earthly king. Also notice the ups and downs that David — the shepherd boy, psalmist, and great warrior — faces before he is anointed as Israel's next king. The books of 1 – 2 Samuel were penned by an unknown author after Israel was divided into northern and southern kingdoms, sometime around 930 BC.

READING

Each day this week, read the passages of Scripture indicated below. If it is helpful, use this chart to help you record your reading progress. Establish a reading schedule that works best for you — and then stick with it. Try to make it a habit to pray before you begin reading each day, asking God to use his Word to instruct and guide you. If you find you are behind in your reading, set aside extra time this week to catch up.

Day	Passage	☑
1	Joshua 1 – 9	☐
2	Joshua 10 – 12; 21:43 – 24:33; Judges 1 – 2	☐
3	Judges 3 – 4; 6 – 7; 10:29 – 39; 13 – 16; 21:25	☐
4	Ruth 1 – 4; 1 Samuel 1; 2:12 – 26; 3 – 6; 8	☐
5	1 Samuel 9 – 11; 13:1 – 15; 15 – 18; 23 – 24; 31	☐

STUDY QUESTIONS

1. What are some of the highlights — knowledge gained, puzzling questions, moments of insight — you experienced during your reading this week?

2. How did God encourage Joshua to be faithful? What words did God speak, and what promises did God make to him (see Joshua 1:9)? How did Joshua respond to God?

3. How did God use Joshua to fulfill his promises to Israel (see Joshua 21:43 – 45)? What does this tell us about the nature of God?

4. In what ways was God willing to help the Israelites conquer the land? What did the Israelites fail to do? How did God respond to this failure?

5. What does Judges 21:25 tell us about the condition of the hearts of God's people during the time of the judges? How does the story of Ruth give us a glimmer of hope for them? Who was part of Ruth's family line (see Ruth 4:17)?

6. How would you describe Samuel's relationship with God? In what ways did God use him from an early age to minister to the Israelites?

7. Why did the Israelites want Samuel to choose a king for them (see 1 Samuel 8:19 – 22)? What was God's response? In what ways were they rejecting him?

8. Why was David God's choice for king? What does the story of Goliath tell us about David's relationship with God (see 1 Samuel 17:37)? What can we learn about God from this story?

Use the space below to write down any key points or questions you want to bring to the next group meeting.

A Brief Survey of
Joshua – 1 Samuel

Keep this Book of the Law always on your lips; meditate on it day and night, so that you may be careful to do everything written in it. Then you will be prosperous and successful.

JOSHUA 1:8

WELCOME

Welcome to session 4 of *A Brief Survey of the Bible*. Take a few minutes to go around the group and invite everyone to answer the following questions:

- How has our culture's esteem of faithfulness in relationships changed over the years?
- What elements of our culture distort the way in which God presents himself in the Bible?

READING FOLLOW-UP

1. What challenges did you face in getting your reading done? What was the most effective thing you did to meet those challenges?

2. As you read the Bible this week, what particular thoughts and/or events stood out to you or surprised you? Why?

3. What questions came up during your reading for which you'd like to find answers?

WATCH THE VIDEO

Play the video teaching segment for session 4. As you watch, use the following outline to record any thoughts or concepts that stand out to you.

Notes

Joshua is about God's faithfulness in fulfilling the promises he made to give the Israelites the Promised Land of Canaan. But Joshua isn't the hero of this story. God is the hero, for he brought the people into the land and helped them conquer it.

The book of Judges covers hundreds of years. It shows the cycles of unfaithfulness in the Israelites as first they sinned and then God raised up one judge after another to deliver them. God's *faithfulness* continued even in the midst of the *faithlessness* of his people.

The Israelites were struggling with their worldview. They were coming out of a native culture in which the people worshiped many gods, and they often turned to these other gods to resolve the everyday problems with which they didn't want to bother God. It was hard for them to change, just as we also have difficulty in rising above our native culture.

At the end of Joshua there is covenant renewal — again! Through the cycle of failures in the book of Judges, we see that the leadership of the people was not stacking up. At the end of the book it states, "Israel had no king; everyone did as they saw fit" (Judges 21:25).

The story of Ruth takes place during the time of the judges. Ruth is a story of contrast — she showed the faithfulness that God was seeking in his people. From this faithfulness, God would build the line of David.

The book of 1 Samuel lays the groundwork for kingship. Samuel was God's instrument — the one who was going to crown the king. It was important for the author to clearly show that Samuel was God's man so it would also be clear that David was God's man. God chose Samuel especially for this task. We see Samuel's dedication and his godliness, and how God blessed him.

The people thought their problem as a nation was a political problem, but it was actually a spiritual problem: their unfaithfulness. They sought a political solution and insisted they wanted a king like the other nations around them. As a result God gave them Saul, who looked the part of a king but proved to be a failure.

David and Goliath is a "God story." David saw clearly that it was God's job to fight the Israelites' battles, and the winner was going to be the one whose God was the strongest. David knew that if God was stronger, then anyone could go fight Goliath — even *he* could fight.

God's idea of a king was one who went forth in his power and ruled in his power. He wanted a man who would be willing to be used as his instrument. David would prove to be a king according to God's own desires.

GROUP DISCUSSION

Take a few minutes with your group members to discuss what you just watched and explore these concepts in Scripture.

1. As you watched the video, which particular points stood out to you? Which aspect of the video most enhanced your understanding of what you read this past week?

2. How is God the hero of the story of Joshua? What do the stories of the conquest of Canaan tell us about the people God wants to use to accomplish his purpose?

3. What consequences did the Israelites experience for not destroying the Canaanites and removing their gods from the land? What does this reveal about how sin works in our lives?

4. In the book of Judges we find a repeating cycle in which the people sinned, God raised up a judge, the people turned toward obedience, and then they fell away as soon as that judge died. What does the story of Ruth tell us about God's sovereign will and how he enables his promises to be fulfilled? How have you seen God do this today?

5. What did the Israelites' request for a king show about their relationship with God? What happens when we don't recognize our own sin and look for solutions outside of God's plan?

6. The Israelites had a difficult time breaking away from the culture of their day. Why is it also difficult for us to stand apart from ungodly influences in our culture?

7. What is the difference between being an *instrument* of God and being an *obstacle* to God's working in our lives and in the lives of people we influence?

8. What characterized David's faith and relationship with God at this point in his life? What was it about David that God was looking for in a leader? What is God looking for in his people today?

LIVING THE WORD

For this activity each group will need pictures that represent the current culture, scissors, glue sticks, markers, and a large sheet of paper.

––––––◦◦◦◦◦––––––

Work with a small group of people to use the pictures provided to create a collage that describes your culture. Identify those things in your world that tend to pull you away from God — obstacles to a growing, thriving relationship with him. Look for subtle influences, not just the obvious red flags. What ungodly influences have crept into your relationships with others, your work ethic, your parenting, and how you handle your finances? What is one thing God can help you do to overcome those influences? Pray together about each of these challenges.

CLOSING PRAYER

Use the following prayer to close out your group time, or feel free to say one of your own.

> Lord, you are all-powerful, all-knowing, and always with us. Help us recognize your presence and rely on your strength. May we boldly declare you are King and serve you with faithful confidence, knowing that the battle belongs to you. It is a privilege to be your instrument in the world today. Amen.

Did You Know?

- The Israelites entered Canaan, the territory we know as the coast of modern Lebanon and Israel, in about 1250 BC — during what biblical archaeologists call the Late Bronze Age. Although none of the powerful nations of the ancient Near East — Egypt, Babylon, Assyria — had a strong presence in Canaan at that time, the Canaanites were extensive traders. Thousands of artifacts unearthed in ancient sites reveal that Canaanite culture was quite advanced and in many ways superior to that of Israel. (*NIV Study Bible* and *Zondervan Handbook to the Bible*)

- Just how much trouble did Samson cause for the Philistines? Consider the fact that in order to entice Delilah to trap Samson, each of the five Philistine rulers offered her 1,100 shekels of silver — a sum that was equivalent to the price of 275 slaves. (*NIV Study Bible*, note on Judges 16:5)

- Moab, where Ruth grew up, was located east of the Dead Sea and west of the desert along both sides of the Arnon River gorge. The Moabites, who were descendants of Lot's first son, did everything they could to block Israel's expansion. The king of Moab hired the prophet Balaam to curse Israel (see Numbers 22 – 24); Moabite women drew Israelite men into immorality (see Numbers 25); and Chemosh, the Moabites' primary god, proved to be a strong lure for them. Even King Solomon built a sacred site for Chemosh worship on a hill east of Jerusalem, which resulted in God's judgment and the divided kingdoms of Israel and Judah (see 1 Kings 11:10 – 13). (*NIV Study Bible*)

On Your Own
Between-Sessions
Personal Study

This week, you explored God's story in the books from Joshua – 1 Samuel. In the next session, you will be discussing key stories and principles from the books of 2 Samuel – 2 Kings. Use the following between-sessions material to give you some background on these books and guide your reading for the week.

OVERVIEW

The following is a brief overview of the books you and your group will cover during next week's session. Take a moment to review this information, and at the end of the section note any questions you want to discuss with your group.

2 Samuel

The book of 2 Samuel continues the story of Israel as they transitioned from the time of the judges to the monarchy, beginning with the death of King Saul and David's ascension to the throne. The book depicts the most magnificent high points of David's forty-year reign, as well as the low points of his life and that of his family. David's affair with Bathsheba — an ugly story of lust, abuse of power, deceit, and murder — was but a preview of what would follow. In fulfillment of Nathan's prophecy that David's sin with Bathsheba would split the house of David, we see the consequences unfold, bringing division and suffering not only to David's household but to the entire nation of Israel.

1 Kings

The book of 1 Kings picks up where 2 Samuel left off and provides a history of the kingship in light of God's covenants. Note the brutal causes and effects of the rebellion after Solomon's death that splits Israel into two kingdoms. At times this parallel structure can make it a bit challenging to keep it all straight, as you witness the succession of kings from both Israel (the kingdom in the north) and Judah (the kingdom in the south). Pay attention to which kings do "right in the eyes of the LORD" and which ones don't, and notice how God responds. Both the books of 1 – 2 Kings were written by an unknown author around 550 BC, during the time of the Israelites' exile in Babylon.

2 Kings

The book of 2 Kings continues the story of the two kingdoms (it was originally one literary work, just like 1 – 2 Samuel and 1 – 2 Chronicles). As you read, imagine what it would have been like for God's people who repeatedly compromised with evil until they faced God's judgment. Notice how the prophets Elijah and Elisha respond as they try to guide the people back toward God. Watch for the destruction of Jerusalem, which is the climax of the Old Testament's plot.

READING

Each day this week, read the passages of Scripture indicated below. If it is helpful, use this chart to help you record your reading progress. Establish a reading schedule that works best for you — and then stick with it. Try to make it a habit to pray before you begin reading each day, asking God to use his Word to instruct and guide you. If you find you are behind in your reading, set aside extra time this week to catch up.

Day	Passage	☑
1	2 Samuel 2 – 3; 5 – 8; 11 – 12	☐
2	2 Samuel 13 – 17; 1 Kings 1 – 3; 6	☐
3	1 Kings 8 – 9; 11 – 12; 14 – 17	☐
4	1 Kings 18 – 19; 21 – 22; 2 Kings 1 – 2; 4 – 6	☐
5	2 Kings 9 – 10; 12; 17 – 18; 22 – 25	☐

STUDY QUESTIONS

1. What are some of the highlights — knowledge gained, puzzling questions, moments of insight — you experienced during your reading this week?

2. How did God help David during the early days of his reign as king? How would you describe David's relationship with God at this time?

3. What did God promise David in 2 Samuel 7 (see especially verses 9, 11 – 16)? How would you describe David's reign as king after his sin with Bathsheba?

4. Solomon started out his reign as an instrument of God, but he made choices throughout his time on the throne that eventually led to his fall. In what areas did he do according to God's plan and in what areas did he fail?

5. What happened to David's kingdom after Solomon's death? Who were some of the kings who did right in the eyes of the Lord? What did they do that pleased God? What was the primary sin of the kings who did evil?

6. How did God encourage the prophet Elijah in his faith? How would you describe Elijah's relationship with God? How would you describe his courage to obey God?

7. Elisha followed in Elijah's footsteps. In what ways did Elisha help the people? What dangers did he encounter in his stand for God's ways?

8. Although there were a few kings — including Joash, Hezekiah, and Josiah — who honored God, the vast majority led the people astray. How was God keeping his promise by allowing them to be sent into exile (see 1 Kings 9:6 – 9)?

Use the space below to write down any key points or questions you want to bring to the next group meeting.

A Brief Survey of
2 Samuel – 2 Kings

As for God, his way is perfect: The LORD's word is flaw-less; he shields all who take refuge in him. For who is God besides the LORD? And who is the Rock except our God?

2 SAMUEL 22:31 – 32

WELCOME

Welcome to session 5 of *A Brief Survey of the Bible*. Take a few minutes to go around the group and invite everyone to answer the following questions:

- When you are planning a household project, how do you determine what tools and resources you will need to do the job well?
- What qualities do you look for in a strong leader? Why those qualities?

READING FOLLOW-UP

1. What challenges did you face in getting your reading done? What was the most effective thing you did to meet those challenges?

2. As you read the Bible this week, what particular thoughts and/or events stood out to you or surprised you? Why?

3. What questions came up during your reading for which you'd like to find answers?

WATCH THE VIDEO

Play the video teaching segment for session 5. As you watch, use the following outline to record any thoughts or concepts that stand out to you.

Notes

When God made a covenant with Abraham, he was revealing himself through a family that he had chosen. When God gave the Law at Sinai, he was revealing his character, his holiness, to his people. Now he is going to reveal his kingship over the nation.

In bringing David to the throne, God was showing the Israelites what his kingship was like. God's presence was not just passive — he was active in bringing order to this world.

At the beginning of David's reign, we see that he served as an instrument of God. Later, when we read stories such as the episode with Bathsheba, we see that David was not the kind of instrument he should have been. He became an *obstacle*.

David began to abuse his power — adultery and murder were just symptoms of this. David did not pass down the values of the covenant from father to son, and David allowed foreign influences to invade the land. We see this pattern of failure throughout the kings that follow.

One highlight in the books of 1 – 2 Kings is the few kings who *did things right*. Another is the *building of the temple* as a permanent place for God's presence. Through Israel, God brought about a dwelling place on earth. All the nations on the earth would be blessed through Israel, because God's revelation and presence would come through that nation.

Unfortunately, most of the kings did evil, and the prophets had to call them to accountability. Elijah and Elisha were two such prophets who showed what God's kingship should be like. Elijah was God's champion against Baal, and God used him to show the people who was in charge. Elisha operated as a substitute king, providing justice for the people and bringing victory in battle as the Lord worked through him.

The failures of the kings and the people resulted in their exile from the Promised Land. The books of 1 – 2 Kings were written during the time of the exile — from the perspective of what went wrong and how the people's unfaithfulness to the covenant had led to this mess.

GROUP DISCUSSION

Take a few minutes with your group members to discuss what you just watched and explore these concepts in Scripture.

1. As you watched the video, which particular points stood out to you? Which aspect of the video most enhanced your understanding of what you read this past week?

2. God blessed David's early reign because David relied on him and honored his Law. In what ways does God bless those who honor him today? What are some ways God uses faithful people as his instruments?

3. David's sin affected not only his own family and the people close to him but also the entire nation. How does our sin affect people beyond ourselves? How does it affect their relationships with God?

4. The books of 1 – 2 Kings show that God is sovereign over all events and can even use as instruments those who are not following his ways. How have you seen God accomplish his purposes through people who do not acknowledge him? How does this remind you that God is in control of everything in your life?

5. The prophets Elijah and Elisha show us it can be difficult to be faithful to God. What costs did they have to pay for being obedient to God? What might following God cost you?

6. Israel went into exile because of their unfaithfulness to God. How did God use this consequence to bring the people back into relationship with him? How does God use the consequences of sin to encourage us to remain faithful to him?

7. Even though the Israelites had committed great acts of evil, the Lord still provided them with a way to keep his covenants while they were in exile. Knowing God's Word and nourishing a relationship with him were key in the lives of those who tried to be faithful. How can knowing God's Word and prayer help you stand strong in faithfulness to God?

8. What did you learn from these Scripture passages about God and the relationship he desires to have with you?

LIVING THE WORD

For this activity, group members will need a blank notebook or journal and a pen.

As you have been preparing for these sessions, you have been establishing a habit of daily Bible study. Knowing the Bible is the first step in building a relationship with God that will endure. Being obedient to follow his ways allows you to see his presence in your life. This week, in addition to your daily Bible study, cultivate a time of prayer with God by using your notebook to write down your prayers. Record the date and the Scripture passage you are reading at the top of the page, and then ask God to speak to you through what you are reading. Record any insights you receive in response to your prayers, and then share these insights with someone else in your group. Finally, take time to reread your prayers; it will build your faith to see how God reveals himself in response to your prayers!

CLOSING PRAYER

Use the following prayer to close out your group time, or feel free to say one of your own.

> *Thank you, God, that you reveal yourself to us through your Word and through our circumstances. You are passionate about drawing us closer to you, and we are thankful that you never give up on us. We ask that you help us to remove those things in our lives that have become obstacles in our relationship with you, and we ask for your forgiveness. Help us to recognize the impact our faith has on others, and may we be instruments for your purposes. Amen.*

Did You Know?

- After the nation of Israel split into two separate kingdoms, none of the nineteen kings of Israel did what was right in the eyes of God. So God allowed Assyria to defeat Israel in 722 BC, and none of the scattered survivors appears in history after that time. Of the nineteen kings of Judah, only a handful worked to guide the people toward God. So God allowed the Babylonians to destroy Judah and take its people to Babylon in 586 BC.

- Jerusalem, the city King David established as Israel's capital, was first populated during the third millennium BC. The fortress-like city sat on a hill, with deep valleys on three sides, and received water from an underground source. The tribes of Judah and Benjamin attacked the city during the conquest of Canaan and set the city on fire, but the Jebusites later recaptured it (see Joshua 15:63). The Israelites didn't control Jerusalem until about 1000 BC, when it is believed David captured it by entering through a tunnel that brought water into the city. At that time the city was quite small — smaller than eleven acres in size and with no more than 3,500 people. Strategically located on the border of Israel and Judah, Jerusalem's location helped David unite both kingdoms without showing favor to either one. (*Zondervan Handbook to the Bible* and *NIV Study Bible*, note on 2 Samuel 5:6)

- God promised to establish David's "house" — a royal dynasty — that would last forever (see 2 Samuel 7:11 – 16). Ultimately, God fulfilled his covenant with David through the kingship of Jesus Christ, who was born of the house of David of the tribe of Judah. (*NIV Study Bible*, note on 2 Samuel 7:11)

On Your Own
Between-Sessions
Personal Study

This week, you explored God's story in the books from 2 Samuel – 2 Kings. In the next session, you will be discussing key stories and principles from the books of 1 Chronicles – Nehemiah. Use the following between-sessions material to give you some background on these books and guide your reading for the week.

OVERVIEW

The following is a brief overview of the books you and your group will cover during next week's session. Take a moment to review this information, and note at the end of the section any questions you want to discuss with your group.

1 Chronicles

The book of 1 Chronicles was written for the exiles who had returned to rebuild Jerusalem under Ezra and Nehemiah. In this book, the author (possibly Ezra) traced the genealogy and interpreted the history of God's people (primarily from 1 – 2 Samuel and 1 – 2 Kings). As you read, notice an emphasis on the political and spiritual events of David's reign and the covenant promises God was keeping by establishing David as Israel's king. The books of 1 – 2 Chronicles were composed sometime between 450 and 400 BC.

2 Chronicles

The book of 2 Chronicles records the deeds of the kings of Judah who came after Solomon. Pay attention to how often the phrases "was fully committed to the LORD" (15:17) or "did evil in the eyes of the LORD" (21:6) appear, as they illustrate what really matters to God (and what should matter to us as well). Throughout the books of 1 – 2 Chronicles there are frequent references to outside sources lost to time, including "the book of the kings of Israel" (2 Chronicles 20:34) and prophetic writings by "Samuel the seer" (1 Chronicles 29:29) and "Ahijah the Shilonite" (2 Chronicles 9:29).

Ezra

The book of Ezra relates how God's covenant people were restored from Babylonian exile to the land of Israel. Ezra, a priest and scribe, is believed to have arrived in Jerusalem in the seventh year of the reign of Persian king Artaxerxes I (458 BC), followed by Nehemiah, who arrived in the king's twentieth year of rule. Notice how God uses Ezra to restore Israel's identity among the Jewish exiles. Also note how Ezra challenges the people — who have spent decades in Persian society disregarding God's Law and mixing worship of the God of the covenant with worship of foreign gods — to fully uphold God's Law. Ezra is believed to have penned the book sometime after 440 BC.

Nehemiah

The book of Nehemiah describes the events that transpired after the first waves of Israelites returned to the land. In particular, it shows how God used Nehemiah — a cupbearer for the Persian king Artaxerxes I — to rebuild the walls of Jerusalem and protect it from enemies. As you read, you will see how God used Nehemiah's prayers, plans, and passion to accomplish great things. In the end, Nehemiah not only led the people to reconstruct the wall around Jerusalem but also helped restore Jewish tradition and faithfulness to God in the community. It is believed the author/compiler of Ezra and Nehemiah was also the author of 1 – 2 Chronicles.

READING

Each day this week, read the passages of Scripture indicated below. If it is helpful, use this chart to help you record your reading progress. Establish a reading schedule that works best for you — and then stick with it. Try to make it a habit to pray before you begin reading each day, asking God to use his Word to instruct and guide you. If you find you are behind in your reading, set aside extra time this week to catch up.

Day	Passage	☑
1	1 Chronicles 1 – 3; 5; 9 – 11; 13 – 15	☐
2	1 Chronicles 16 – 18; 21 – 22; 28 – 29; 2 Chronicles 1 – 2	☐
3	2 Chronicles 3; 5; 7:11 – 22; 9:13 – 31; 12; 29 – 32; 36	☐
4	Ezra 1; 3 – 7; 10:1 – 17; Nehemiah 1 – 2	☐
5	Nehemiah 3 – 4; 6:1 – 7:3; 8 – 9; 10:28 – 39; 12:27 – 13:31	☐

STUDY QUESTIONS

1. What are some of the highlights — knowledge gained, puzzling questions, moments of insight — you experienced during your reading this week?

2. How did God reveal his presence with David as he was establishing his kingship (see 1 Chronicles 11:9 – 10)? How did David rely on God during this time?

3. Through David's successes and failures, he recognized his need for God's power and presence. What advice did David give to his son Solomon when he talked to him about building the temple (see 1 Chronicles 22:11 – 13; 28:20 – 21)?

4. How was God's presence manifest when Solomon brought the ark of the covenant into the temple (see 2 Chronicles 5:7 – 14)? What promises and warnings did God give Solomon when the building projects were completed (see 7:12 – 22)?

5. What challenges did the people face during Ezra's day in their attempt to rebuild the temple (see Ezra 4)? What did they do in the face of these obstacles? How did God use these situations to help them rebuild (see Ezra 5 – 6)?

6. What sin did Ezra see in the people's lives? Why was it important for them to deal with this issue, given the effect it had had in Israel's history (see Ezra 9 – 10)?

7. How did Nehemiah encourage the people when they experienced opposition from enemies such as Sanballat (see Nehemiah 4:11 – 15)? When the wall was finished, what did Ezra and the people do (see Nehemiah 8 – 10)? Why was ethnic purity so vital to the nation's existence (see Ezra 10 and Nehemiah 9)?

8. Nehemiah made sure God's Law was being obeyed in Jerusalem. What corrections and reforms did he command in Nehemiah 13?

Use the space below to write down any key points or questions you want to bring to the next group meeting.

6

A Brief Survey of
1 Chronicles – Nehemiah

If my people, who are called by my name, will humble

themselves and pray and seek my face and turn from

their wicked ways, then I will hear from heaven, and I

will forgive their sin and will heal their land.

2 CHRONICLES 7:14

WELCOME

Welcome to session 6 of *A Brief Survey of the Bible*. Take a few minutes to go around the group and invite everyone to answer the following questions:

- What are some destructive patterns of behavior you see in people's lives today? What are some positive patterns?

- How can a person break an old habit and build a new one?

READING FOLLOW-UP

1. What challenges did you face in getting your reading done? What was the most effective thing you did to meet those challenges?

2. As you read the Bible this week, what particular thoughts and/or events stood out to you or surprised you? Why?

3. What questions came up during your reading for which you'd like to find answers?

WATCH THE VIDEO

Play the video teaching segment for session 6. As you watch, use the following outline to record any thoughts or concepts that stand out to you.

Notes

The books of 1 – 2 Chronicles were written 150 years after 1 – 2 Kings, so there is a sense of expectation that comes from their perspective on history.

The authors of 1 – 2 Chronicles were looking for patterns to give hope to the exiles. They saw that when the people and kings were unfaithful to God, there was judgment. But when the people and kings were faithful — when they kept the Law and were obedient to its commands — God did wonderful things.

The pattern told the chronicler that the kingdom of God was not just about a king. The most important part of God's kingdom was *spiritual*. Until the people got the spiritual part straightened out, they couldn't expect the political part to work out.

Ultimately the people rebuilt the temple, and God was again in their midst. They also rebuilt Jerusalem, put the Law in place, and formed a new community identity. They were no longer focused on a king and needed the spiritual leadership of the priests and Levites.

Ezra took the responsibility of establishing the Law as the foundation of society. Nehemiah took the responsibility of rebuilding the walls of Jerusalem.

The emphasis in the books of Ezra and Nehemiah is God showing how he was instrumental in restoring his people. After two generations, God regathered an exiled and dispersed people and provided a means for them to come back to the covenant land. God used Persian emperors giving decrees and money to help God's people return and rebuild the temple and the walls.

Nehemiah bathed the whole process in prayer, and we see how God worked through those prayers. We also see that God ruled over the greatest empires of the world, as king after king fell into God's program.

No matter what choices people make, whether good or bad, God can fold them into his plan. This doesn't mean God lets the bad off the hook, but he can use anything to accomplish his purposes. That is the God who reveals himself in these pages of Scripture.

GROUP DISCUSSION

Take a few minutes with your group members to discuss what you just watched and explore these concepts in Scripture.

1. As you watched the video, which particular points stood out to you? Which aspect of the video most enhanced your understanding of what you read this past week?

2. What does 1 – 2 Chronicles tell us about the importance of remaining faithful to God? What are some healthy patterns of behavior that can help you focus on being faithful?

3. How did God show the people they belonged to him? What are some ways that God shows believers in Christ that they are his children?

4. What qualities of God's kingdom did you see illustrated in the events of rebuilding the temple and the walls of Jerusalem? How do repentance, dedication, reading God's Word, and prayer help you see what God's kingdom is like?

5. How did the people respond when they recognized their unfaithfulness to God's Law? What are ways people today respond when they know they have done something wrong? What kinds of responses please God?

6. In what ways did Nehemiah demonstrate his reliance on God and his deep commitment to prayer? What does a life bathed in prayer look like today?

7. What does the picture of God ruling over the empires of the world reveal to us about his plans? What perspective does this give you when looking at your own circumstances?

8. How does the picture of God presented in these Scriptures often differ from what you see presented about him today?

LIVING THE WORD

For this activity, group members will need a pen and a strip of card stock that measures 2" x 11".

———— ⊗ ————

Work with another group member to create a list of words that describes God as portrayed in 1 – 2 Chronicles, Ezra, and Nehemiah. Write the words in a column on your strip of card stock, review your list together, and share how you have seen God express himself in each of the ways you have listed. Circle any words that are not part of your experience with God. How can adding these missing aspects give you a fuller understanding of who God is? Why is it important to have a clear picture of how God is presented in Scripture? What are the dangers of having a lopsided picture of God? Keep your list in your Bible and add to it as you continue to explore and study the Scriptures.

CLOSING PRAYER

Use the following prayer to close out your group time, or feel free to say one of your own.

Lord, you work through any situation to accomplish your purposes. You are the King of Kings and the Ruler of all! We thank you that we can have a relationship with you and experience your love, forgiveness, correction, and guidance. Please give us the wisdom and strength we need to never compromise your Word. Thank you that we can have hope and confidence in you. Amen.

Did You Know?

- The fall of Jerusalem represents the climactic point of Old Testament history. The book of Nehemiah, though it is not the end of the Old Testament, covers the final events in Old Testament history. The remaining books of the Old Testament either fill in information along the previous timeline or provide an artistic, philosophical, or prophetic view of the events that have transpired in Israel's history.

- Ezra took on an unpopular issue when he spoke out against mixed marriages between God's people and heathen people. God forbade such marriages because they led to idolatry, yet even priests, kings, and Levites had done it. Some of the men had even broken marriages to Jewish wives in order to marry idol-worshiping women (see Malachi 2:10 – 16).

- Nehemiah was a cupbearer to the Persian king, and it was his duty to serve the drinks at the royal table. Due to the constant threat of plots and intrigues, the king had to have a great deal of trust in the person assigned to this role. Nehemiah showed himself trustworthy and, as a result, was able to gain the ear of the king. When Nehemiah set out from the Persian winter capital of Susa, about 200 miles east of Babylon, he traveled about 1,100 miles to reach Jerusalem. (*Zondervan Handbook to the Bible*)

On Your Own
Between-Sessions
Personal Study

This week, you explored God's story in the books from 1 Chronicles – Nehemiah. In the next session, you will be discussing key stories and principles from the book of Esther through the first half of the book of Psalms. Use the following between-sessions material to give you some background on these books and guide your reading for the week.

OVERVIEW

The following is a brief overview of the books you and your group will cover during next week's session. Take a moment to review this information, and at the end of the section note any questions you want to discuss with your group.

Esther

The book of Esther is named after its principle character, a young Jewish exile who married the Persian king Xerxes. As you read the story, try putting yourself in her position. Watch her faith in God grow, and notice how God uses her courageous actions and those of Mordecai to save the Jews from annihilation. Consider, too, that Esther lived in Persia about thirty years before the events recorded in Nehemiah. The author of Esther is unknown, but his knowledge of Persian customs and lack of references to conditions in Judah indicate he was a resident of a Persian city. The book was likely written sometime after 460 BC.

Job

Job is the first book in what is known as the "books of poetry." The books vary in literary form and cover a wide range of functions, from wisdom literature to personal prayers and hymns of worship. As you read Job, pay close attention to the scenario set up in this book, which probably took place during the time of Abraham, Isaac, and Jacob. Also reflect on the insights into the nature of suffering and faith, who God is and how deeply he values righteousness, and the unseen spiritual conflicts between God's kingdom and Satan's kingdom.

Psalms 1 – 90

The title "Psalms" refers to songs that were sung to the accompaniment of instruments such as the harp, lyre, and lute. The book is a collection of songs that were written across several centuries, with the earliest written about the time of Moses (1440 BC) and the time following the Babylonian exile (after 538 BC). The psalms are organized into separate books: (1) Psalms 1 – 41, (2) Psalms 42 – 72, (3) Psalms 73 – 89, (4) Psalms 90 – 106, and (5) Psalms 107 – 150. While reading the poetic prayers and hymns in this book, note those that especially connect with you. You'll want to return to them for further reading at a later date. Pay close attention to what the psalms reveal about faith, godliness, hope, justice, and God being at the center of life.

READING

Each day this week, read the passages of Scripture indicated below. If it is helpful, use this chart to help you record your reading progress. Establish a reading schedule that works best for you — and then stick with it. Try to make it a habit to pray before you begin reading each day, asking God to use his Word to instruct and guide you. If you find you are behind in your reading, set aside extra time this week to catch up.

Day	Passage	☑
1	Esther 1 – 10	☐
2	Job 1 – 10	☐
3	Job 11 – 12; 27 – 28; 32; 38 – 42	☐
4	Psalms 1 – 3; 5 – 6; 13; 15; 18 – 19; 23 – 25	☐
5	Psalms 30; 33 – 34; 45; 47; 50 – 51; 60; 66; 74; 89 – 90	☐

STUDY QUESTIONS

1. What are some of the highlights — knowledge gained, puzzling questions, moments of insight — you experienced during your reading this week?

2. God is never mentioned in the book of Esther. How do we know that God is working behind the scenes in the lives of Esther, Mordecai, and the Jewish people at this time?

3. What kinds of questions did Job ask God (see Job 12 – 13)? What kind of answer did God provide him (see Job 38:2 – 5)?

4. What did God's answer communicate to Job about his circumstances (see Job 38:36 – 37; 40:1 – 14)? How did Job's attitude toward God change as he dialogued with God and heard the Lord's response (see Job 42:1 – 3)?

5. How was God working in both the lives of Esther and Job? What pictures do these stories give you about God's involvement in people's circumstances?

6. Who is the subject of Psalm 1? On whom does Psalm 2 focus? What circumstances was the psalmist describing in these two psalms?

7. Describe the progression of the psalmist's attitude in Psalms 6 and 13. What does this progression tell you about the writer's picture of God?

8. What do the psalms that you read tell you about God and how he responds to people in crisis?

Use the space below to write down any key points or questions you want to bring to the next group meeting.

A Brief Survey of
Esther – Psalm 90

Come and see what God has done, his awesome deeds
for mankind!... He rules forever by his power, his eyes
watch the nations — let not the rebellious rise up against
him.

PSALM 66:5, 7

WELCOME

Welcome to session 7 of *A Brief Survey of the Bible*. Take a few minutes to go around the group and invite everyone to answer the following questions:

- What kind of training helps a person handle a crisis?
- What questions do people usually ask when faced with a crisis?

READING FOLLOW-UP

1. What challenges did you face in getting your reading done? What was the most effective thing you did to meet those challenges?

2. As you read the Bible this week, what particular thoughts and/or events stood out to you or surprised you? Why?

3. What questions came up during your reading for which you'd like to find answers?

WATCH THE VIDEO

Play the video teaching segment for session 7. As you watch, use the following outline to record any thoughts or concepts that stand out to you.

Notes

In the book of Esther, God was working behind the scenes through events that most casual observers would call "coincidence." The person of faith sees God working out his plan through these kinds of coincidences.

Job and his friends were working under the assumption that justice pervaded the world. For this reason, Job, a righteous man, called God's justice into question. The opening scene in heaven shows us it is God, not Job, who is on trial.

In Job, we see a shift from the question of God's justice to the question of God's wisdom. Once we can see that God is wise, we can accept that he is also just.

Job shows us that even though God set up this world for his presence to be in it, he is not *inside* the system. He is not present in all of the elements of nature. He controls what *happens* in our world, but he is not *in* them.

When things happen to us and we ask why, we can't expect an answer. Job never found out why. We can't explain the cause, but we can ask the *question* of God's purpose. Cause looks to the past, but purpose looks to the future.

When we embrace the picture of God that Scripture gives us, we're prepared to respond to crisis situations. Reading the Bible prepares us for crisis situations. When that crisis comes, when suffering happens, we know what to do — because our picture of God is firmly in place.

The book of Psalms presents the same struggles we saw in Esther and Job. Again, faith is on trial. Psalms works out how God responds in moments of crisis.

In Psalms, we have crisis, deliverance, and praise. Even with the turmoil the psalmist sometimes experiences, the idea is to present a God who rules and is in control.

Psalms 1 and 2 set the course for the entire book. Psalm 1 tells us about the individual who either does what is right or wrong and how God responds. Psalm 2 focuses on a national level, showing nations in tumult and God supporting his anointed king.

GROUP DISCUSSION

Take a few minutes with your group members to discuss what you just watched and explore these concepts in Scripture.

1. As you watched the video, which particular points stood out to you? Which aspect of the video most enhanced your understanding of what you read this past week?

2. Even though the word *God* never appears in Esther, what does the book show us about how God often works in our lives? How does this affect your view of "coincidences" in your life?

3. What does the story of Esther show you about how God uses people to accomplish his purposes? What is your responsibility in responding to the situations God puts in your life?

4. How did Job's relationship with God change when his perspective shifted from why he was suffering to trusting in God's wisdom for his circumstances? What circumstances are you seeking a *cause* for? How can seeking God's *purpose* instead change your relationship with God?

5. What does God's answer to Job tell you about his ability to work in a fallen and sinful world? How does this help you trust that God is just? How does it affect your picture of who God is?

6. When suffering happens in your life, how does your picture of God affect how you respond? How does reading Scripture prepare you for times of crisis?

7. What have the Psalms you have read shown you about God? How has the psalmist helped you rely on God when you are struggling?

8. How are God's sovereignty and kingship key themes of this portion of Scripture? What impact will this make on your life today?

LIVING THE WORD

For this activity, every group member will need a notecard and an envelope.

———⚬⚬⚬———

Every situation is an opportunity to be part of God's work in the world. Today, consider a current struggle that someone close to you is experiencing. How does God want you to personally respond to this situation? Share your thoughts with a partner in your group, and then pray together for God's guidance about how to respond. As God gives you insight, plan one way you can be his instrument to the individual on your heart. Perhaps God is asking you to give of your time to help that person, to use your talents to provide for his or her needs, or to open your home to him or her. Write a note explaining your plan and that you are acting on God's behalf. As appropriate, mail or personally deliver the note to the person, and then start the process of following God's leading in this situation. Recognize that your effort will come at a cost, but that God has you covered. Finally, like the psalmist, give praise and thanks to God for his wisdom and power to work in every circumstance.

CLOSING PRAYER

Use the following prayer to close out your group time, or feel free to say one of your own.

> *Lord, nothing is outside of your reach. Your hand is working in every situation, and we can take confidence in the justice of your cause. Allow us to see opportunities to be your hands and feet in this world and show your love to others. Prepare us to respond in both good times and in crisis with faith in your strength and wisdom. Amen.*

Did You Know?

- God commanded King Saul to execute the Amalekites and their evil king Agag because they were the first people to attack the Israelites after their departure from Egypt (see Exodus 17:8 – 16; 1 Samuel 15:2). But Saul disobeyed God and spared Agag. As it turns out, Haman probably was a descendant of Agag (see Esther 3:1). Using Haman, Satan again tried to destroy God's people and his unfolding plans. At stake was not only the Jews' existence but also the future appearance of Jesus, the Messiah.

- During one of Job's discourses, he refers to a time when, as a healthy man, he took his seat at "the gate of the city" (Job 29:7). This means Job had been an influential leader in his community. During ancient times, the city elders presided over the most important legal cases and administrative business at the city gate — the equivalent of what we would call "city hall." (*NIV Study Bible*, notes for Job 29:7; Ruth 4:1; Genesis 19:1)

- The book of Psalms was collected during a six-hundred-year period from the time of David to the time of Ezra. Some of the psalms clearly point to the coming Messiah, even though they were written a thousand years before Jesus' birth (see Psalms 2; 8; 16; 22; 69; 72; 89). The prophetic nature of the psalms is validated by the New Testament, which references at least seventeen instances where the book of Psalms refers to Christ. (*You Are Here in the Bible*, notes on Psalms)

On Your Own
Between-Sessions
Personal Study

This week, you explored God's story from the book of Esther through the first half of the book of Psalms. In the next session, you will be discussing key stories and principles from the rest of Psalms to Song of Songs. Use the following between-sessions material to give you some background on these books and guide your reading for the week.

OVERVIEW

The following is a brief overview of the books you and your group will cover during next week's session. Take a moment to review this information, and at the end of the section note any questions you want to discuss with your group.

Psalms 91 – 150

Included in this section of Psalms are those known as the "pilgrimage songs" (Psalms 120 – 134). These hymns were often sung by the Jewish pilgrims who were journeying to Jerusalem and the temple. As you read, continue to note psalms that especially connect with you. Consider the many ways the psalmists praise God for who he is and what he has done. Take note of references in the psalms to events about which you already have read (for example, Israel's time in the wilderness, described in Psalm 95:10).

Proverbs

Although the book of Proverbs is closely linked with the wise sayings of Solomon, it is clear from later chapters that there were several authors (likely a circle of wise men). King Lemuel's sayings in Proverbs 31:1 – 9 contain several Aramaic spellings, which may indicate he had a non-Israelite background. As you read these short sayings, note that they are not intended to be taken as prophecy or promises but as general principles for making wise choices in life. The book of Proverbs was likely compiled during Solomon's reign, around 970 – 930 BC.

Ecclesiastes

The unknown "Teacher" of this work (perhaps Solomon) sets the tone with these memorable words: "Utterly meaningless! Everything is meaningless" (Ecclesiastes 1:2). From there, he meanders into an exploration of the meaning and futility of life. As you read, don't miss the subtle theme that somehow — despite the confusion, uncertainty, and pain — there is a God who has placed eternity in our hearts, who desires our love and reverence, and who offers us hope in himself. In addition, notice that while much of the book expresses the futility of a life lived without God, the book's concluding statement is one of hope. The date of composition for Ecclesiastes is unknown, but it could be as early as 1000 BC.

Song of Songs

The Hebrew title for this book is "Solomon's Song of Songs," meaning a song by, for, or about Solomon. From this we derive two titles for this book: "Song of Solomon," as in the *New King James Version*; and "Song of Songs," as in the *New International Version*. The book's celebration of love has often been interpreted in several ways — as an allegory, as wisdom literature, as a love song, or as a combination thereof. As you read, reflect on the images of sexual love, marital fidelity, and the couple's shameless enjoyment of their God-given sexuality. The book is possibly authored by Solomon, who is referenced seven times, and might have been written as early as 1000 BC.

READING

Each day this week, read the passages of Scripture indicated below. If it is helpful, use this chart to help you record your reading progress. Establish a reading schedule that works best for you — and then stick with it. Try to make it a habit to pray before you begin reading each day, asking God to use his Word to instruct and guide you. If you find you are behind in your reading, set aside extra time this week to catch up.

Day	Passage	☑
1	Psalms 94 – 95; 97; 103; 106; 115; 119; 121; 136; 139; 145; 150	☐
2	Proverbs 1 – 4; 10; 16; 21 – 22; 26; 30 – 31	☐
3	Ecclesiastes 1 – 6	☐
4	Ecclesiastes 7 – 12	☐
5	Song of Songs 1 – 8	☐

STUDY QUESTIONS

1. What are some of the highlights — knowledge gained, puzzling questions, moments of insight — you experienced during your reading this week?

2. What are the primary attributes of God you observe in Psalms 94, 97, and 103? What do these attributes tell you about how God relates to his people? How is this comforting? How is this awe-inspiring or unsettling?

3. What relationship is the author describing in Psalm 106? What relationship is he describing in Psalm 139? How does Psalm 145:8 – 13 summarize God's relationship with his people?

4. Why is wisdom important (see Proverbs 1:1 – 7; 2:1 – 22)? How does the author compare the fate of the wicked to that of the wise?

5. The book of Proverbs presents principles for living in the fear of the Lord (see Proverbs 1:7; 2:5). How are *principles* different from *promises*? Compare Proverbs 26:4 and 26:5. Why would it be difficult to see both of these verses as promises?

6. What do you think the writer is advising us to let go of in Ecclesiastes 1:2? What, according to Ecclesiastes 7:15, does he say we should accept?

7. In Ecclesiastes 3:1 – 8, the writer describes the way life is. How is this different from our concept of a normal life? How is this view more realistic?

8. Song of Songs is about wisdom in the area of love and sex. How does the author describe the power of love and sex in Song of Songs 8:6 – 7? How does wisdom gained through "the fear of the LORD" (Proverbs 2:5) bring the power of these forces under control?

Use the space below to write down any key points or questions you want to bring to the next group meeting.

A Brief Survey of
Psalm 91 – Song of Songs

Then you will understand the fear of the LORD and find the knowledge of God. For the LORD gives wisdom; from his mouth come knowledge and understanding.

PROVERBS 2:5 – 6

WELCOME

Welcome to session 8 of *A Brief Survey of the Bible*. Take a few minutes to go around the group and invite everyone to answer the following questions:

- How would you describe what a "normal" life looks like?

- What would you say is the difference between a *principle* and a *promise* in the Bible? Give an example of each.

READING FOLLOW-UP

1. What challenges did you face in getting your reading done? What was the most effective thing you did to meet those challenges?

2. As you read the Bible this week, what particular thoughts and/or events stood out to you or surprised you? Why?

3. What questions came up during your reading for which you'd like to find answers?

WATCH THE VIDEO

Play the video teaching segment for session 8. As you watch, use the following outline to record any thoughts or concepts that stand out to you.

Notes

Psalm 139 tells us that God knows everything about us. When we know God is good and wants the best for us, we are happy to have him know everything about us.

Psalm 145 is the climax of the book. It depicts a personal, compassionate, merciful, forgiving God whose kingdom extends across the earth. This is who we are learning about as we read God's Word — it is his way of telling us who he is.

The book of Proverbs offers generalizations that can be true in some situations, though not necessarily in *all* situations. The wisdom comes in using the wise words in the right situation.

What's different about wisdom in the Bible is that we are told it begins with "the fear of the LORD" (Proverbs 1:7). When everything is put in its proper place, God is there right at the foundation of it. Without him at the center, nothing in our lives will make sense.

The author of Ecclesiastes explores every aspect of life and finds it comes up short — *life means nothing*. Self-fulfillment is not found in wealth, power, family, or religion. He doesn't offer us an alternative way to find self-fulfillment but says to abandon the quest — it's doomed to failure.

What the author of Ecclesiastes is calling us to do is readjust our idea of *normalcy*. Life is a rollercoaster — the ups and downs are *normal* and to be expected — and we go through seasons. We shouldn't expect self-fulfillment (or even pursue it) but just enjoy what God brings our way. In the good times we rejoice and enjoy. In the bad times we learn and grow.

Song of Songs shows us there is power in love and in sex. It is a power that upsets our world and disrupts good relationships and sound thinking. We need to understand the power that love and sex have in our lives, in our world, in our relationships — and we need to harness it.

Wisdom is putting everything in its place — having everything ordered, controlled, and built on the foundation of the fear of the Lord. God created love and sex, and those also need to come under his control in our lives.

GROUP DISCUSSION

Take a few minutes with your group members to discuss what you just watched and explore these concepts in Scripture.

1. As you watched the video, which particular points stood out to you? Which aspect of the video most enhanced your understanding of what you read this past week?

2. In Psalm 139 we read that God is good, loving, and knows everything about us. How does that affect your relationship with him? How does it make you feel to know that God understands *everything* about you and chooses to love you in spite of your flaws?

3. The book of Proverbs offers abundant wisdom and principles for making choices that typically yield desirable outcomes in life. However, why is it important to remember that these outcomes are not necessarily *guaranteed* in every situation?

4. What principle in Proverbs caught your attention? What changes might occur in the world if more people practiced that principle? How might following this wisdom impact your life?

5. How was your perspective of good and bad circumstances in life challenged or changed as you read Ecclesiastes? How do your expectations influence what gives your life meaning? What do you believe is the foundation of true wisdom and a meaningful life?

6. Ecclesiastes and Song of Songs are both attributed to Solomon, but they are very different books. What is the dominant spirit of Ecclesiastes? In contrast, how would you describe the spirit of Song of Songs? How are wisdom and the fear of the Lord part of both books?

7. What do you see as the dominant theme of the Song of Songs? What power do love and sex exert in our lives? How can bringing the power of love and sex under God's control allow us to experience its goodness?

8. Why is it important that Song of Songs is part of Scripture? What wisdom from this book do you need to incorporate in your life? What impact would you like it to have?

LIVING THE WORD

For this activity, each group member will need an 11" x 17" piece of paper, a pen, a Bible, and a concordance or a way to look up verses electronically.

Across the long edges of your paper, write several past ups and downs you have experienced in life. The ups should go along the top of the paper and the downs along the bottom. In the center of the page, write one thing you can rejoice in and/or one thing you learned by going through both the good and bad experiences. Now write a current situation you are handling. What wisdom from God can you incorporate into your response? Look up a few verses that reflect God's wisdom in your specific situation and write those verses by the circumstance. How can this process increase your knowledge of God? As you implement God's wisdom, record how this experience grows your relationship with him.

CLOSING PRAYER

Use the following prayer to close out your group time, or feel free to say one of your own.

> *We thank you, Lord, that you are the source of all wisdom. You look into our lives, see our needs, and offer your wisdom to help us navigate all the ups and downs of life. Draw us closer to you and help us turn to you for insight and understanding. May we have a healthy fear of you that pushes us to walk in obedience, respond to you in love, and know your Word. Amen.*

Did You Know?

- Psalm 114, the "Passover hymn," celebrates the Exodus and probably was composed after Israel and Judah divided. It was likely written for liturgical use at the temple during a religious festival. Scholars consider this hymn to be one of the best-fashioned songs of the Psalter. (*NIV Study Bible*, note for Psalm 114)

- The book of Proverbs frequently uses vivid images from everyday life to communicate important principles. For example, Proverbs 3:15 compares wisdom to rubies, which were the most priceless jewel in the ancient world (see also Proverbs 31:10). In Proverbs 7:16, the adulterous woman says she has covered her bed with "colored linens from Egypt," which were expensive and thus associated with wealth. Proverbs 11:1 refers to scales, on which silver was weighed by balancing against a specific stone weight. Dishonest people improperly labeled their weights. (*NIV Study Bible*, notes for Proverbs 3:15; 7:16; 11:1; 31:10)

- The "sachet of myrrh" mentioned in Song of Songs 1:13 was an aromatic gum derived from balsam trees in India, Ethiopia, and Arabia. Used as a perfume, this gum was also an ingredient in holy anointing oil. In the New Testament, we read that the wise men brought myrrh to Jesus as a gift (see Matthew 2:2, 11).

On Your Own
Between-Sessions
Personal Study

This week, you explored God's story from the second half of the book of Psalms through the book of Song of Songs. In the next session, you will be discussing key stories and principles from the books of Isaiah – Lamentations. Use the following between-sessions material to give you some background on these books and guide your reading for the week.

OVERVIEW

The following is a brief overview of the books you and your group will cover during next week's session. Take a moment to review this information, and at the end of the section note any questions you want to discuss with your group.

Isaiah

Isaiah, whose name means "the LORD is salvation," began his ministry in 740 BC, the year King Uzziah of Judah died (see 6:1). Most of the events in Isaiah 1 – 39 occurred during his ministry, so it is likely he recorded them not long after 701 BC. Isaiah lived until at least 681 BC and may have written the rest of the chapters during his later years (if he indeed was the author, which in recent scholarship has been somewhat in debate). As you read, notice the strong themes of destruction and redemption that occur within the context of the spiritual turmoil of Judah and other nations. (Don't be overly concerned about hard-to-understand visions and prophecies.) Watch for allusions to events you have already read about, such as Sodom and Gomorrah (see Isaiah 1:9). In the later chapters you will discover a message of comfort, encouragement, and a future hope. Pay attention to the praise Isaiah offers to God, the beautiful poetry in chapters 36 – 39, the powerful imagery Isaiah uses, and his words about the coming Messiah.

Jeremiah

Jeremiah began his prophetic ministry in 626 BC, during the time of King Josiah of Judah, and he railed against the sin of God's people for forty years. The book that bears his name was actually recorded by Baruch, his faithful secretary, who wrote down his words sometime between 626 and Jeremiah's death in 586 BC. While the prophet was not popular among his contemporaries, he is the one whom Jesus most often quoted. As you read, notice how often Jeremiah warns the people to stop committing adultery, using perverted worship practices, and turning away from God in general. Jeremiah's persecution and suffering increases as God's judgment approaches — he is actually in chains when the Babylonians take over Jerusalem. Take special notice of Jeremiah's role as God's messenger to the remnant who are not taken away to Babylon. Consider what happens to them and how God responds to nations that have battled his people.

Lamentations

As you read this poetic book, try to imagine the Jewish people's loss over the destruction of Jerusalem in 586 BC at the hands of the Babylonians. Not only have the people's city and temple been destroyed, but they have also been exiled from the homeland God had given them. Although God ordained their punishment, notice the hope, love, faithfulness, and salvation he continues to offer. The author of Lamentations is not known, though tradition ascribes it to Jeremiah. It was written sometime after the fall of Jerusalem, between 586 – 516 BC.

READING

Each day this week, read the passages of Scripture indicated below. If it is helpful, use this chart to help you record your reading progress. Establish a reading schedule that works best for you — and then stick with it. Try to make it a habit to pray before you begin reading each day, asking God to use his Word to instruct and guide you. If you find you are behind in your reading, set aside extra time this week to catch up.

Day	Passage	☑
1	Isaiah 1 – 2; 6 – 12; 14	☐
2	Isaiah 24 – 27; 36 – 40	☐
3	Isaiah 42 – 43; 50 – 53; 55; 61; 65 – 66	☐
4	Jeremiah 1 – 4; 7; 9; 18 – 19; 27 – 29; 32	☐
5	Jeremiah 36 – 40; 43; 50; 52; Lamentations 1; 3 – 4	☐

STUDY QUESTIONS

1. What are some of the highlights — knowledge gained, puzzling questions, moments of insight — you experienced during your reading this week?

2. What did God say to Ahaz through Isaiah when Jerusalem was threatened (see Isaiah 7:7 – 9)? How did Ahaz respond to God (see verses 12 – 13)? Refer to 2 Kings 16 and 2 Chronicles 28 for background on these events. What do God's efforts through Isaiah tell you about his interest in his people?

3. Isaiah gives us a picture of God's ideal king (see Isaiah 9 and 11) — qualities that were lacking in most of the kings of Judah. What do these qualities tell you about God? These qualities also describe a future king — the root of Jesse (King David's father), the ancestor of Jesus. How do you think the words of Isaiah gave hope to the people when all seemed lost? (Refer to Matthew 1:18 – 23 and 2:17 for more about Jesus' fulfillment of Isaiah's prophecies.)

4. Isaiah also spoke to King Hezekiah when Sennacherib, the king of Assyria, was threatening Jerusalem (see Isaiah 36 – 37). How was Hezekiah's response different from Ahaz's? Refer to 2 Kings 18 – 19 and 2 Chronicles 32 for background on these events. What message do these events give us about placing our trust in God?

5. Jeremiah lived about a hundred years after Isaiah, as Babylon was coming into power over the Assyrians. In Jeremiah 7:1 – 15, what warning does the prophet give to the people in Jerusalem about their worship practices? What efforts had God made to help them correct their ways? What was the most devastating consequence of their unfaithfulness?

6. What does Jeremiah say will happen to Jerusalem because of their persistence in sin (see Jeremiah 9:11)? How does God feel about their sin? How does he feel about the destruction they will experience?

7. Lamentations 1 and 4 were written to mourn the destruction in Jerusalem and the exile of many of the people. How are the city and land described? How is Jerusalem a reminder to the people of their rebellion (see Lamentations 1:18)?

8. How would you describe the people's relationship with God at this time? How does this compare to the relationship God offered them through the covenant with Moses (see Jeremiah 7:22 – 23; Exodus 6:2 – 8)? What glimmer of hope do we find in Lamentations 3:19 – 33? What is it about the character of God that makes this hope possible?

Use the space below to write down any key points or questions you want to bring to the next group meeting.

9

A Brief Survey of
Isaiah – Lamentations

"For I know the plans I have for you," declares the LORD, "plans to prosper you and not to harm you, plans to give you hope and a future. Then you will call on me and come and pray to me, and I will listen to you. You will seek me and find me when you seek me with all your heart."

JEREMIAH 29:11 – 12

WELCOME

Welcome to session 9 of *A Brief Survey of the Bible*. Take a few minutes to go around the group and invite everyone to answer the following questions:

- As citizens of our country, we each enjoy certain privileges. But on what are those privileges dependent? What do we need to do to maintain them?
- What are some of the feelings we experience when we lose someone's presence in our lives? How does that loss affect us?

READING FOLLOW-UP

1. What challenges did you face in getting your reading done? What was the most effective thing you did to meet those challenges?

2. As you read the Bible this week, what particular thoughts and/or events stood out to you or surprised you? Why?

3. What questions came up during your reading for which you'd like to find answers?

WATCH THE VIDEO

Play the video teaching segment for session 9. As you watch, use the following outline to record any thoughts or concepts that stand out to you.

Notes

The messages of the prophets reveal what God expects of us and what he is like. The prophets arose during times of crisis in Judah and Israel to serve as God's representatives and spokespersons to the people.

The Assyrian empire was growing in power during Isaiah's time. Ahaz, the first king mentioned in the book, was faced with a military situation. Unfortunately, he chose to rely on other countries and his own efforts rather than obey Isaiah's message to trust God. His plans failed.

However, King Hezekiah listened to Isaiah when he was faced with the armies of Sennacherib, the king of Assyria. Because he chose to obey, Jerusalem was miraculously delivered.

Isaiah prophesied about an ideal king who was coming and would be a perfect representative of God's kingship. This ideal king, from David's line, came to be referred to as the Messiah — one who would come and rule in God's name.

One of the first names given to this Messiah was *Immanuel*. This name means "God with us," one who would represent God's presence in a person. This is a new stage of God's presence among his people. (In the New Testament, Jesus was born and called Immanuel.)

Isaiah spoke his words around 700 BC, when the exile was still a couple of hundred years away (in 586 BC). Later, the people in exile could look back at Isaiah's words and find hope in them. They knew that God was not finished with them yet.

Jeremiah ministered a century after Isaiah. At this point history was at a transition between the Babylonians and the Assyrians, and the nation of Israel was experiencing a spiritual moment of reform. Yet Jeremiah warned Israel about the threat of Babylon from the north.

Jeremiah warned the people about the possibility of their losing God's presence. In fulfillment of his words, the place of God's presence (the temple) was knocked down because of the people's sin and disobedience. They had been given an incredible privilege in being God's chosen people, but they lost that privilege when God's presence departed.

GROUP DISCUSSION

Take a few minutes with your group members to discuss what you just watched and explore these concepts in Scripture.

1. As you watched the video, which particular points stood out to you? Which aspect of the video most enhanced your understanding of what you read this past week?

2. What does Isaiah teach us about God's holiness and our need for his redemption and restoration? What are some cycles of sin that we need to break today?

3. A prophet is a representative of God during a time of crisis. How would you feel if God called you to be a public advocate for him today, as were the prophets Isaiah and Jeremiah? How would your relationship with God help you accomplish what he asked you to do? How does your relationship with God need to grow in order for you to be prepared for such a calling?

4. What were some of the differences between Ahaz and Hezekiah? What is our responsibility in dealing with the circumstances and crises that impact our lives?

5. The Israelites blended idol worship with worship at God's temple. How do ungodly attitudes still creep into our worship and attitude toward God today? In what ways do Christians often take God's presence for granted?

6. Even in the midst of utter destruction, God provided hope through the promise of a king — the Messiah. How has God provided for his presence to be manifest in your life? How can you enjoy that privilege?

7. How does reading the prophetic words of Scripture and seeing their fulfillment inspire hope in you? How do these words give you a more accurate picture of God and his sovereignty?

8. In what ways has God used events and circumstances to call you back to him? How have you responded?

LIVING THE WORD

For this activity, group members will need a six-inch clay pot, a permanent marker, several small stones, water, some potting soil, and flower or vegetable seeds.

———— ∞∞ ————

Our relationship with God requires daily commitment and nourishment on our part. God provides his presence and power, but we must provide an environment for God's presence to take root. On the outside of the flower pot, write down some specific commitments you need to make for God's presence to grow in your life. Next, place a few small stones in the bottom, add soil, and plant three to four seeds as directed on the package. Add just enough water to moisten the soil. Provide a place in your home where your seeds have the best opportunity to thrive. When you see them, remember that we can create an environment for seeds to grow, but without God's intervention they will never germinate and sprout. Also take a moment to pray and ask God to bring growth and understanding in your relationship with him.

CLOSING PRAYER

Use the following prayer to close out your group time, or feel free to say one of your own.

> *Your presence is precious to us, Lord. You hold our lives, our circumstances, and our future in your hands. Thank you for your Word, for the courage of prophets such as Isaiah and Jeremiah, and for the wisdom they give us. May we be receptive to your direction and be ready to respond with boldness. Amen.*

Did You Know?

- The role of the Old Testament prophet was not to give people a blueprint of future events but to encourage them to live in the way God wanted — a way that reflected their relationship to him. The prophets were responsible to speak the things God had given them to say, but the listeners had responsibilities too. They were responsible to hear and heed the things said to them, turn their faith into action, and live out the justice and holiness and love of their God. They were also responsible for assessing whether or not the prophet was really speaking from God, for being honest with themselves, and for not trying to bribe the prophet to give nice warm messages that only contained things they wanted to hear (see Isaiah 30:10 – 11; Jeremiah 5:31). (*Zondervan Handbook to the Bible*)

- Some of Isaiah's prophecies related to imminent events, not just distant events. For example, in Isaiah 10:24 – 27, he predicted that God would annihilate the Assyrian army. This occurred in 701 BC. (*NIV Study Bible*, note for Isaiah 9:4)

- At the time Isaiah prophesied against the city of Babylon, its beautiful temples and palaces were world renowned. In fact, the hanging gardens of King Nebuchadnezzar (605 – 562 BC) were one of the seven wonders of the ancient world. The city boasted canals, numerous monuments, a staged temple tower 295 feet high, and city walls wide enough that a four-horse chariot could turn around on top of them. (*NIV Study Bible*, note for Isaiah 13:19)

- Jeremiah's life and struggles are shown to us in greater depth and detail than those of any other Old Testament prophet. His name most likely means "the LORD throws," either in the sense of hurling the prophet into a hostile world or of throwing down nations in divine judgment for their sins. (*NIV Study Bible*)

THE PROPHETS IN THEIR PLACE			
Book	Date of Writing	Audience	Theme(s)
Isaiah 1 – 39	c. 701 BC	Judah	Judgment against Judah and Israel; prophecies of promise and blessing; judgments against nations.
Isaiah 40 – 55	before 680 BC	Judah	Deliverance and restoration of Israel; the servant's ministry; God's call to salvation.

Isaiah 56–66	before 680 BC	Judah	Condemnation of wicked; worship; restoration; everlasting deliverance, everlasting judgment.
Jeremiah	c. 626–586 BC	Judah	Warnings and exhortations; his suffering; fall of Jerusalem; judgment against nations.
Lamentations (Jeremiah)	after 586 BC	Judah	Laments over destruction of Jerusalem.
Ezekiel	c. 593–571 BC	Jews in Babylon	God's sovereignty over creation, people, nations, and history; God's holiness; judgment against Judah and pagan nations; God's future work in history.
Daniel	c. 530 BC	Jews in Babylon	Prayer, spiritual warfare, living by God's standards in a hostile environment, God's sovereignty.
Hosea	after 721 BC	Israel	Just as Hosea is betrayed by his beloved, God is betrayed by his beloved Israel. Loving commitment can overcome betrayal.
Joel	c. late 7th to early 5th centuries BC	Judah	God's people have a choice: keep doing wrong and be judged, or repent and receive God's forgiveness and salvation.
Amos	c. 760–750 BC	Israel	Social justice as the indispensable expression of true piety; God's judgment; God's sovereignty.
Obadiah	c. 605–586 BC	Judah	God's judgment against the Edomites, who are gloating over Jerusalem's destruction.
Jonah	c. 750–725 BC	Israel/nations	Jonah represents the Israelites' jealousy of their favored relationship with God and unwillingness to share his compassion with other nations.
Micah	c. 700–650 BC	Israel and Judah	God's judgment and deliverance; warnings against idolatry and rebellion; triumph of God's kingdom.
Nahum	before 612 BC	Judah/nations	Lord's judgment on Nineveh.
Habakkuk	c. 605 BC	Judah	Arguments with God over his unfathomable ways; God's reply; prophet's confession of faith.
Zephaniah	c. 640–627 BC	Judah	The coming Day of the Lord, when God will punish the earth; God's mercy to his people.
Haggai	520 BC	Post-exilic Jews in Judah	A call for the complacent people of Judah to resume rebuilding the temple to give glory to God.
Zechariah	c. 520–480 BC	Post-exilic Jews in Judah	Encouragement and motivation for the discouraged exiles to complete rebuilding the temple.
Malachi	c. 430 BC	Post-exilic Jews in Judah	Assurances the Messiah will come not only to judge his people but also to bless and restore them.
Sources: *Zondervan Handbook to the Bible, NIV Study Bible*			

On Your Own
Between-Sessions
Personal Study

This week, you explored God's story in the books from Isaiah – Lamentations. In the next session, you will be discussing key stories and principles from the books of Ezekiel – Malachi. Malachi is the last book in the Old Testament. Use the following between-sessions material to give you some background on these books and guide your reading for the week.

OVERVIEW

The following is a brief overview of the books you and your group will cover during next week's session. Take a moment to review this information, and at the end of the section note any questions you want to discuss with your group.

Ezekiel

The book of Ezekiel contains some of the strangest imagery in the Bible. However, though parts of it can be difficult to understand, pay attention to the constant theme that God is sovereign over nations, people, history, and all creation. As you read, consider why God repeats variations of "then they will know that I am the LORD." Notice, too, the theme of holiness and what Ezekiel predicts concerning God's design of redemption that will unfold in the New Testament. The book was written between 593 – 571 BC to the Jews who had been taken captive to Babylon.

Daniel

Daniel was a young man of Judah who was taken into captivity by the Babylonians. From the first pages of the book, he stands out as a leader — both spiritually and politically. Take note of the qualities of his relationship with God, including his faithfulness, his trust in God, and his commitment to prayer. Consider also the repeating theme of God's sovereignty over all people. The book was written around 530 BC and contains two separate parts: a historical narrative (Daniel 1 – 6) and prophetic literature (Daniel 7 – 12), which would have served as an encouragement to the people of God in exile.

Hosea

Hosea is the first of what are known as the Minor Prophets, so named because of the shorter books they wrote. Hosea lived during the final days of the northern kingdom of Israel and likely wrote the book after that kingdom's fall to Assyria in 722 – 721 BC. Hosea stands out because God used his life — not just his words — as a symbol of his love for his people.

Joel

Little is known about the prophet Joel, but it is likely he lived in Judah and wrote sometime between the late seventh and early fifth centuries BC. His message was that God's restoration and blessing would come only after the Lord's judgment (the "Day of the Lord") and the people's repentance. Peter would later quote from the prophet during his sermon on the day of Pentecost (see Acts 2:16 – 21).

Amos

Amos was a shepherd and keeper of a sycamore-fig grove who likely prophesied from 760 – 750 BC. Although he lived in Judah, his book was targeted to the idolatrous people of the northern kingdom of Israel. Amos's dominant theme is a call for social justice (see 5:24). He also speaks of God's judgment of all nations and the Lord's love, grace, mercy, and forgiveness. He refers to God as the Great King who rules the universe (see 9:5 – 6).

Obadiah

Little is known of Obadiah, the author of this shortest book in the Old Testament, though it is likely he ministered during the time of the Babylonian attacks against Jerusalem in 605 – 586 BC. His message is one of judgment against Edom (Esau's line) for that nation's failure to assist Israel and for its people's gloating over Jerusalem's destruction.

Jonah

Jonah is believed to have prophesied from 793 – 753 BC to the northern kingdom of Israel, though the book was likely written down after the exile, perhaps between 750 – 725 BC. The focus of this entertaining and well-known story is not only on God's mercy to the people of Assyria but also on the Israelites' reluctance to accept that compassion to their enemies.

Micah

Micah lived in southern Judah and prophesied from 750 – 686 BC. The theme of his book is God's judgment and deliverance. He stresses that God hates idolatry, injustice, rebellion, and empty ritualism but delights in pardoning the repentant.

Nahum

Little is known of Nahum, who prophesied between 663 – 612 BC to the people of Judah. The focus of his book is on the Lord's judgment of Nineveh (Assyria) for the people's oppression, idolatry, and wickedness. Nahum points out God's sovereignty as the Lord of history and all the nations.

Habakkuk

Habakkuk likely lived in Judah toward the end of King Josiah's reign from 640 – 609 BC, or at the beginning of Jehoiakim's reign from 609 – 598 BC. His message is unique in that it is a dialogue between himself and God — a sort of wrestling match with the Creator over his unfathomable ways. Yet the prophet's dialogue results in a new confession of faith as he learns to trust in God and work with him in a spirit of worship.

Zephaniah

Zephaniah was a man of social standing in Judah who was related to the royal line (he was a fourth-generation descendant of King Hezekiah). He ministered during the time of King Josiah from 640 – 609 BC. His theme focuses on the coming "Day of the Lord" — a time when God will punish the nations for their sin, including the nation of Judah. However, like other prophets, he ends his pronouncement of doom on the positive note that Judah will one day be restored.

Haggai

Haggai was the first of three Minor Prophets who ministered to the exiled Jews who had returned to the land of Israel. It is possible that he witnessed the destruction of Solomon's temple in 586 BC and was in his seventies at the time of his ministry. His writing can be precisely dated at 520 BC, during the second year of King Darius of Persia. Haggai's primary message was on the consequences of disobedience and obedience and the blessings the people would receive if they gave priority to God and rebuilding his house, the temple.

Zechariah

Zechariah, like Jeremiah and Ezekiel before him, was a member of a priestly family. He was born in Babylon and was among the exiles who returned to Judah in 538/537 BC. Like Haggai, his main purpose for writing to the post-exilic Jews is to compel them to complete the rebuilding of the temple. Zechariah also foretells Christ's coming and emphasizes that God will be faithful to his people if they choose to return to him.

Malachi

Malachi ministered to the exiles in Judah during the time of Nehemiah and likely wrote his book during Nehemiah's return to Persia in 433 BC or during his second period as governor. His aim is to rebuke the people for doubting God's love and to call them to return to honoring the Lord. He states God is coming not only to judge his people but also to bless and restore them.

READING

Each day this week, read the passages of Scripture indicated below. If it is helpful, use this chart to help you record your reading progress. Establish a reading schedule that works best for you — and then stick with it. Try to make it a habit to pray before you begin reading each day, asking God to use his Word to instruct and guide you. If you find you are behind in your reading, set aside extra time this week to catch up.

Day	Passage	☑
1	Ezekiel 1 – 5; 10; 12:1 – 16; 24; 37:1 – 14; 40 – 43; 48:30 – 35	☐
2	Daniel 1 – 6; 10; 12; Hosea 1; 3; 14; Joel 2	☐
3	Amos 5; 7; Obadiah; Jonah 1 – 4; Micah 5 – 7; Nahum 1 – 3	☐
4	Habakkuk 1 – 3; Zephaniah 1 – 3; Haggai 1 – 2	☐
5	Zechariah 1 – 2; 6 – 8; 14; Malachi 1 – 4	☐

STUDY QUESTIONS

1. What are some of the highlights — knowledge gained, puzzling questions, moments of insight — you experienced during your reading this week?

2. Ezekiel and Daniel both wrote during the time of the Jews' exile in Babylon. What picture do you see in these books of God's power over the nations? What words of warning and hope do you see? How was the faith of Ezekiel and Daniel tested?

3. What common theme do you see in the books of Hosea, Joel, Amos, and Obadiah? What response was God looking for from his people? What do these Scriptures tell you about the relationship God wants to have with his people?

4. The book of Jonah isn't about the prophet Jonah but about what God is seeking when people are confronted with their sin. What was Jonah's basic message? How did the people of Nineveh respond? How did God feel about their response?

5. What future for God's kingdom do you see in these prophetic Scriptures? In light of the destruction and suffering the people experienced because of their sin, what did this message of a future tell them about God (see Micah 7:14 – 19; Zephaniah 3:9 – 17; Haggai 2; Zechariah 8:1 – 13; Malachi 3:16 – 18)?

6. How do the prophets describe the relationship God has with those who are unrighteous? How do they describe God's relationship with those who turn to him and repent?

7. In Malachi 3:6, God talks about his commitment to his covenant with Jacob. In other prophetic Scriptures, the authors recount God's faithfulness throughout the history of his people. Why was it important for the people to be reminded of the covenant and God's sovereign hand in history?

8. In Ezekiel 43, God said Jerusalem and the temple would be rebuilt and that his presence would return among his people. This prophecy was fulfilled when the Jews began to return to Israel under the Persians. What challenges did they face once they returned? How did the prophets Haggai, Zechariah, and Malachi motivate them to return to God?

Use the space below to write down any key points or questions you want to bring to the next group meeting.

10

A Brief Survey of
Ezekiel – Malachi

He has shown you, O mortal, what is good. And what

does the LORD require of you? To act justly and to love

mercy and to walk humbly with your God.

MICAH 6:8

WELCOME

Welcome to session 10 of *A Brief Survey of the Bible*. Take a few minutes to go around the group and invite everyone to answer the following questions:

- What conditions allow for a healthy relationship to thrive?
- How do difficult situations test a relationship with another person?

READING FOLLOW-UP

1. What challenges did you face in getting your reading done? What was the most effective thing you did to meet those challenges?

2. As you read the Bible this week, what particular thoughts and/or events stood out to you or surprised you? Why?

3. What questions came up during your reading for which you'd like to find answers?

WATCH THE VIDEO

Play the video teaching segment for session 10. As you watch, use the following outline to record any thoughts or concepts that stand out to you.

Notes

The key theme in the book of Ezekiel is the presence of God. Without God's presence, the people are doomed to be exiled.

Ezekiel also presents the theme of God revealing himself through his activities in history. We come to know God when we are exposed to all the things he does in our world. God's goal is for us to *know* that he is the Lord (see Ezekiel 12:16).

Daniel was an instrument of God and serves as an example of faith under trial. The book of Daniel presents the power of God over the empires and the nations of the world, and how they come to recognize God's kingdom and praise him.

The Minor Prophets have a common theme of how people respond to God and his messengers.

After a series of events, Jonah eventually gave a message of destruction to the people of Nineveh. They didn't know exactly *how* to respond to his message, so they responded in a way they knew — and God delivered them. The book of Jonah makes it clear that God wants people to take small steps in the right direction. The Ninevites did this, and God approved.

Malachi lived during the end of the Old Testament period. His message to the exiles was about fixing those things that still needed work.

God made us for relationship so we might know him. Relationship happens when we *respond* to God.

After this period of time we know as the Old Testament, God's presence would take a new step in our world. God would soon provide a new level of relationship that would last forever. Through the thousands of years of history in the Old Testament, God had been building this plan — so that by the time we get to the New Testament, we can know God.

GROUP DISCUSSION

Take a few minutes with your group members to discuss what you just watched and explore these concepts in Scripture.

1. As you watched the video, which particular points stood out to you? Which aspect of the video most enhanced your understanding of what you read this past week?

2. Ezekiel shows us the importance of God's presence in the lives of the people of Israel. What does God's presence look like in your life? What would your life look like without his presence?

3. God interacted with his people throughout the Old Testament and revealed his character and power to them. What event in history comes to mind when you think of God's hand at work? How have you seen God's power and presence in your personal history? How are the words of Ezekiel 12:16 true in your life?

4. The book of Daniel recounts several events in which the faith of Daniel and his friends was put on trial. How did their responses reveal their view of God? How has your faith been tested? How does your picture of God measure up to the one presented in Daniel?

5. Which of Daniel's personal characteristics stand out to you? Why? What can we learn from Daniel's example about faithfully following and serving God in a hostile culture?

6. The people of Nineveh are a great example of a people responding to God's message. They took the message to heart, fasted, called on God, and turned from their ways. What does their example show us about how to respond to God? What can you learn from them?

7. As you've studied God's messages through prophets such as Malachi, what have you learned about making godly changes in your life? Where do you still have work to do?

8. What happens to our relationship with God when we listen to his Word and respond in faith? How does this help us when God asks us to endure difficult circumstances or make painful decisions?

LIVING THE WORD

For this activity, everyone will need a piece of paper and pencil.

———— ⌘ ————

God chose prophets in the Old Testament to share specific messages with the people, but it was the responsibility of the people and their leaders to respond to those messages. Gather in groups of two to three people and prayerfully consider what messages of repentance the Bible may have for you. As you pray, be open to what God has been putting on your heart as you have studied his Word, and create a list of areas in which you need to make changes. Make a commitment within your group to support each other and provide accountability as you make progress — for as Scripture demonstrates, relying on God and godly friends are key to success.

CLOSING PRAYER

Use the following prayer to close out your group time, or feel free to say one of your own.

> *Lord, your presence in our lives is precious. You rule the nations, yet you offer us your presence every day. We are humbled by your love, awed by your power, and grateful for your mercy. Help us as we seek to obey your Word. May we be worthy, through your strength, to be living examples of your love. Amen.*

Did You Know?

- The phrase "son of man" is used ninety-three times in the book of Ezekiel to emphasize the prophet's humanity, but the phrase is used only as a proper title in the book of Daniel. In Daniel's vision recorded in 7:13 – 14, he saw the Son of Man as a heavenly figure whom God will entrust with glory, authority, and sovereign power during the end times. A few centuries later, Jesus used this term eighty-one times to describe himself, thus showing that he was the eschatological figure of whom Daniel spoke. (*NIV Study Bible*, notes for Ezekiel 2:1 and Mark 8:31)
- Although God exiled the Israelites from their Promised Land because of their

---

long-term disobedience, he never abandoned his covenant people. Interestingly, God continued to call them by the name "Israel" — their covenant name (see Ezekiel 2:3; 3:4 – 5:7). Even during their captivity, God continued to unfold his redemptive plan. (*NIV Study Bible*, note for Ezekiel 2:1 – 3:15)

- Old Testament prophets often used the term *prostitution* to describe God's disobedient people. But the usage didn't refer only to the act of sexual prostitution or even idolatry. Sometimes it referred to Israel's alliances with pagan nations and preoccupation with worldly politics, such as placing confidence in their own skills and ability to find security rather than completely relying on God. (*NIV Study Bible*, note for Ezekiel 23:5)

- Malachi was likely the last prophet of the Old Testament era (though some place Joel later). For the next four hundred years — what some historians refer to as the "silent years" — we have no new God-inspired writings, although a collection known as the Apocrypha (Greek for "hidden") was composed during this time. The next prophet to appear on the scene would be John the Baptist, who began his ministry in AD 26. (*NIV Study Bible*)

BETWEEN THE TESTAMENTS TIMELINE

Era	Date	Event
Persian Period (450 – 330 BC)		
	430	The book of Malachi is written
	399	Socrates condemned to death in Greece for heretical teachings
	391	The Romans subjugate the Etruscans
	359	Artaxerxes III becomes king of Persia
	359	Philip II becomes king of Macedonia
	355	Alexander the Great is born
	340	Philip II conquers Thrace
	338	Philip II defeats Athens and Thebes and unites Greece under his rule
	336	Darius III becomes king of Persia
	336	Alexander becomes king after Philip II is assassinated
	335	Aristotle teaches in Athens
	334	Alexander begins his campaign in the East
	331	Alexander defeats Darius III and captures the Persian Empire

Hellenistic Period (330 – 166 BC)		
	323	Alexander dies
	320	Ptolemy I Soter captures Jerusalem
	311	Seleucus I conquers Babylon and founds Seleucid dynasty
	305	Ptolemy I is proclaimed king in Egypt
	285	Ptolemy II Philadelphus becomes king of Egypt
	264	First Punic War between Rome and Carthage
	261	Antiochus II Theos becomes king of Syria
	250	Hebrew Scriptures translated into Greek (the Septuagint)
	246	Seleucus II Callinicus becomes king of Syria
	246	Ptolemy III Eurgetes becomes king of Egypt
	241	First Punic War ends
	223	Antiochus III the Great becomes king of Syria
	221	Ptolemy IV Philopater becomes king of Egypt
	218	Second Punic War between Rome and Carthage
	218	Hannibal crosses Alps
	215	Hannibal is defeated by Romans
	205	Ptolemy V Epiphanes becomes king of Egypt. The Rosetta Stone, recording his ascension, is carved.
	203	Second Punic War ends
	198	Judea becomes part of the Seleucid Empire
	187	Seleucus IV Philopator becomes king of Syria
	183	Hannibal commits suicide
	175	Antiochus IV Epiphanes becomes king of Syria
	167	Antiochus IV attacks Jerusalem, sacrifices a pig in the temple, outlaws Jewish religious rites and traditions, and orders worship of Zeus
	166	The Jews, under the leadership of Judas Maccabeus, successfully rebel against Antiochus IV
Hasmonean Period (166 – 63 BC)		
	165	The temple is repaired and cleansed
	160	Judas Maccabeus dies; his brother, Jonathan, leads the Jews
	157	Judea becomes an independent principality
	149	Third Punic War begins between Rome and Carthage
	146	Rome destroys Carthage
	143	Simon Maccabeus becomes leader of the Jews

	141	Judea becomes an independent kingdom
	134	John Hyrcanus becomes leader of the Jews
	130	The Pharisees emerge as a Jewish sect
	103	Aristobulus I declares himself king of Judea
	102	Alexander Janneus becomes king of Judea
	90	Revolt of the Pharisees
	75	Salome Alexandra becomes queen of Judea, with Hyrcanus II as high priest
	70	Virgil is born in Rome
	67	Civil war breaks out in Judea between Hyrcanus II and Aristobulus II
	65	Roman general Pompey invades Syria
	65	Horace is born in Rome
	64	Pompey captures Jerusalem and annexes Syria and Judea
Roman Period (begins in 63 BC)		
	61	Julius Caesar wins his first victories in Spain
	60	First Triumvirate in Rome (Caesar, Crassus, and Pompey)
	53	Crassus is killed
	51	Cleopatra VII becomes joint ruler of Egypt with her brother
	50	Rivalry between Caesar and Pompey
	47	Pompey dies in Egypt
	47	Cleopatra becomes sole queen in Egypt
	47	Antipater becomes procurator of Judea
	44	Caesar is assassinated in Rome
	43	Second Triumvirate in Rome (Octavian, Mark Antony, Marcus Lepidus)
	43	Birth of Ovid
	40	Parthians conquer Jerusalem
	40	Mark Antony appoints Herod the Great king of Judea
	30	Mark Antony and Cleopatra commit suicide
	27	Octavian takes title of Augustus and becomes first emperor of Rome
	19	Herod the Great begins to rebuild temple
	4	Herod the Great dies
	4	Jesus is born in Bethlehem

Sources: *NIV Study Bible* and *Bible-History.com*

On Your Own
Between-Sessions
Personal Study

This week, you explored God's story in the books from Ezekiel – Malachi. In the next session, you will move into the New Testament and discuss key stories and principles from the book of Matthew. Use the following between-sessions material to give you some background on this book and guide your reading for the week.

OVERVIEW

The following is a brief overview of the book you and your group will cover during next week's session. Take a moment to review this information, and at the end of the section note any questions you want to discuss with your group.

Matthew

Although the first gospel in the New Testament is anonymous, the early church was unanimous in its view that it was authored by Matthew (also known as Levi), the tax collector whom Jesus called to be his disciple. Matthew was a Jew who wrote his gospel to other Jewish believers around AD 60 in order to proclaim Jesus as the promised Messiah, the King of the Jews. He shows how Jesus came to fulfill the Old Testament but also to judge the Jews for their unfaithfulness (his gospel strongly condemns the hypocritical Pharisees). Although many stories and events recorded in Matthew are found only in this gospel, perhaps the most noteworthy is Jesus' Sermon on the Mount (see Matthew 5 – 7).

READING

Each day this week, read the passages of Scripture indicated below. If it is helpful, use this chart to help you record your reading progress. Establish a reading schedule that works best for you — and then stick with it. Try to make it a habit to pray before you begin reading each day, asking God to use his Word to instruct and guide you. If you find you are behind in your reading, set aside extra time this week to catch up.

Day	Passage	☑
1	Matthew 1 – 7	☐
2	Matthew 8 – 12	☐
3	Matthew 13 – 17	☐
4	Matthew 18 – 23	☐
5	Matthew 24 – 28	☐

STUDY QUESTIONS

1. What are some of the highlights — knowledge gained, puzzling questions, moments of insight — you experienced during your reading this week?

2. The book of Matthew begins with the genealogy of Jesus (see Matthew 1:1 – 17). Why would this be important to the Jews reading these words?

3. John the Baptist was a prophet similar to those we encountered in the Old Testament. What was John's primary message? What words of hope and warning did he proclaim? How did Jesus fulfill these prophecies?

4. What are some instances in Matthew in which Jesus referred to his fulfillment of an Old Testament prophecy? How do these fulfillments show God's sovereignty?

5. Jesus represents the center point of history. How do we see God's presence with his people change through Jesus?

6. Matthew is one of four accounts about Jesus' life, death, and resurrection. Why is it important for us to have these multiple accounts about Jesus?

7. Matthew's gospel presents a teaching from Jesus that is commonly referred to as the Sermon on the Mount (see Matthew 5 – 7). How would you describe the moral standard Jesus presents in this sermon? Whom does Jesus describe as being blessed (see Matthew 5:3 – 12)? What does this tell us about God's part in making us his holy and blessed people?

8. In what ways would Matthew's presentation of Jesus have been good news, especially to his Jewish readers?

Use the space below to write down any key points or questions you want to bring to the next group meeting.

11

A Brief Survey of
Matthew

All this took place to fulfill what the Lord had said through the prophet: "The virgin will conceive and give birth to a son, and they will call him Immanuel" (which means "God with us").

MATTHEW 1:22 – 23

WELCOME

Welcome to session 11 of *A Brief Survey of the Bible*. In this session, we will begin to explore the New Testament by examining the book of Matthew. Take a few minutes to go around the group and invite everyone to answer the following questions:

- What would people think about you if the only photo they ever saw was your driver's license picture?

- What typically happens when several different people give an account of an event they witnessed together?

READING FOLLOW-UP

1. What challenges did you face in getting your reading done? What was the most effective thing you did to meet those challenges?

2. As you read the Bible this week, what particular thoughts and/or events stood out to you or surprised you? Why?

3. What questions came up during your reading for which you'd like to find answers?

WATCH THE VIDEO

Play the video teaching segment for session 11. As you watch, use the following outline to record any thoughts or concepts that stand out to you.

Notes

The Old Testament can be summed up in the word *promise* — the promise God gave to Adam and Eve, Abraham, and David. The New Testament can be summed up in the word *fulfillment* — God's promise of salvation is coming to fulfillment in Jesus Christ.

The Old Testament points *forward* toward the coming of Jesus. The New Testament points *back* to what Jesus did when he came and accomplished salvation, and then points *forward* to Christ's ultimate return. Jesus is the center point of human history.

John the Baptist is a key transitional figure in the Bible. He was the last of the Old Testament prophets and the herald for the Messiah. We could say that John has one foot in the age of promise and one foot in the age of fulfillment.

The word *gospel* means "good news." The Gospels contain the best news in human history — that Jesus Christ is the Savior of the world.

Each of the Gospels was written in a particular Christian community to address the specific needs and concerns of that community. The Holy Spirit wanted us to have four unique perspectives on Jesus Christ. All of them capture a picture of Jesus. Each takes a different angle and brings out different aspects of who he was and what he came to accomplish.

In Matthew, Jesus is portrayed as the Messiah, the king of the Jews, who came to fulfill prophecy and establish God's reign. In Mark, Jesus is portrayed as the humble servant who suffered and died to pay the penalty of humankind's sins. In Luke, Jesus is portrayed as the Savior — not just for the Jews but for all people. In John, Jesus is portrayed as the divine Son of God, who uniquely reveals who the Father is and who is truly God.

Matthew opens his gospel with Jesus' genealogy. Matthew's readers would have been excited to see that Jesus was the son of David and the son of Abraham. They knew this meant God would restore creation to what it once had been. The Savior had arrived!

As you read the Gospels, look for the portrait of Jesus contained in each one.

GROUP DISCUSSION

Take a few minutes with your group members to discuss what you just watched and explore these concepts in Scripture.

1. As you watched the video, which particular points stood out to you? Which aspect of the video most enhanced your understanding of what you read this past week?

2. Why is it significant that Matthew emphasized Jesus' identity as the Messiah and the King of the Jews? Why was it important for him to show how God was fulfilling his promises of salvation through Christ? Why was this good news for more than just the Jewish people?

3. In what ways have you benefited from your Old Testament reading? How has it prepared you for what you read in Matthew? How has your relationship with God been affected by God's provision of Jesus as the Messiah?

4. What role has the Holy Spirit played in presenting God's Word to us? How does the presence of four Gospels reinforce the message God proclaims to us in his Word?

5. As Jesus taught his disciples, he repeatedly referred to or quoted from Old Testament passages of Scripture. Why do you think he did this? How has your knowledge of Scripture helped you share God's plan of salvation with someone else?

6. When Jesus taught, he often emphasized the importance of a heart commitment rather than mere obedience to man-made rules and traditions. Why was this such a critical truth for his Jewish audience to understand? What does this mean in terms of your commitment to a relationship with God?

7. What would you identify as the key themes of this portion of Scripture?

8. What impact will what you've just seen make on your life today?

LIVING THE WORD

For this activity, you will need several songs (such as "Mighty to Save" and "This I Believe" by Hillsong, or music from other Christian artists) that emphasize God's plan of salvation through faith in Christ, as well as a device to play these songs for the group. You will also need paper and a pen for each person.

As you listen to the music, reflect on what you have learned about God's plan of salvation through Jesus. On your paper, write a statement about what it means to be a Christian based on what you have learned from Scripture. How does what the Bible says line up with your faith in Christ? Do you have any beliefs that aren't biblical? Next, consider what you would say if you were to share with an unbeliever how to find salvation through Christ. Using only five or six sentences, write God's plan of salvation in everyday terms. Finally, practice sharing about Christ with a partner in your group. As you go through your week, consider who in your circle might be ready to hear about Jesus' plan for his or her life.

CLOSING PRAYER

Use the following prayer to close out your group time, or feel free to say one of your own.

> Jesus, thank you for being the fulfillment of God's plan to bring restoration and salvation to our world. Your message is one of good news — the best news — and it should be shared with everyone. We ask for your help through the Holy Spirit to share this message with those who need a relationship with you. Thank you for the opportunities you will bring our way. Amen.

Did You Know?

- The temple in Jerusalem was destroyed in 586 BC when the Babylonians captured Jerusalem. In 19 BC, Herod the Great began a massive reconstruction project on the same site as the temples built by Solomon and Zerubbabel. Known as Herod's temple or the second temple, it was the place where the Jews of Jesus' day came to worship God. The temple's Holy Place and Most Holy Place had the same floor dimensions as the temple Solomon built. It lasted only until AD 70, when the Roman general Titus tore it down after the great Jewish revolt erupted in AD 66. (*NIV Study Bible; Zondervan Handbook to the Bible*)

- In Matthew, the star of Bethlehem that pinpointed Jesus' location had newly appeared, traveled slowly, and "stood over" Bethlehem. According to scholars, only a comet with a long tail could satisfy these criteria. Chinese astronomers, who closely watched stars and comets, observed a spectacular comet that appeared in 5 BC and remained visible for more than seventy days. Data from the Chinese records indicates that the Magi would first have seen this comet in the east, just as Matthew described. (*Zondervan Handbook to the Bible*)

- Matthew included nine proof texts in his gospel to show that Jesus Christ fulfilled the Old Testament Scriptures (see 1:22 – 23; 2:15; 2:17 – 18; 2:23; 4:14 – 16; 8:17; 12:17 – 21; 13:35; 27:9 – 10). He also focused on Jesus' role as "Son of David" in such verses as 1:1, 9:27, 12:23, 15:22, and 20:30 – 31. These help show that Jesus fulfilled the covenant God made with Abraham in Genesis 12:2 – 3 and 15:9 – 21. (*NIV Study Bible*, note for Matthew 1:1)

- By the first century AD, the Jews had divided into several sects, each with its own beliefs and traditions regarding the Law. One dominant sect, the Pharisees, strictly adhered to legalistic traditions. They tried to reinterpret the Law of Moses so that, given all the changes since Moses' day, they could live righteously before God. They believed in angels, demons, the resurrection of the dead, and immortality. (*NIV Study Bible*, note for Acts 15:1)

- The Sadducees, the dominant ruling sect of the time, controlled the temple's organization (including the high priesthood) and the Sanhedrin (the Jewish Supreme Council). They were exacting in Levitical purity and interpreted the Mosaic Law more literally than the Pharisees. They rejected belief in angels, demons, the resurrection of the dead, and immortality. Other groups included the Essenes, who lived a communal monastic lifestyle at Qumran; the Herodians, who supported the government of the Herodian family in Judea; and the Zealots, a revolutionary group who opposed the Roman occupation of Israel. (*NIV Study Bible*)

On Your Own
Between-Sessions Personal Study

This week, you explored God's story in the book of Matthew. In the next session, you will be discussing key stories and principles from Mark – Acts 8. Use the following between-sessions material to give you some background on these books and guide your reading for the week.

OVERVIEW

The following is a brief overview of the books you and your group will cover during next week's session. Take a moment to review this information, and at the end of the section note any questions you want to discuss with your group.

Mark

The early church recognized the author of this gospel to be John Mark, the same man who accompanied Paul and Barnabas on their first missionary journey (see Acts 13:5, 13). Papias of Hierapolis (c. AD 140), quoting an earlier source, stated that Mark was a close associate of Peter, and it is believed Mark compiled his gospel from Peter's preaching and testimony. Mark's account moves rapidly from one episode in Jesus' life to another, emphasizing more what he did than what he said. Mark also stresses how Jesus taught his disciples that the "Son of Man" must suffer and be rejected, and that they must be prepared to walk the same path. It is likely Mark penned his gospel around AD 55.

Luke

Luke, a physician and traveling companion of Paul, was a Greek who wrote his gospel to other Greeks (between AD 60 – 80) to proclaim Jesus as the perfect man. The gospel is a companion volume to Acts, also written by Luke, and is addressed to an individual known as "Theophilus" (see Luke 1:3; Acts 1:1). Luke presents the works and teachings of Jesus that are most essential for understanding the way of salvation. He also focuses on the grace of God as revealed in Jesus and given to those who seem least worthy in society to receive it.

John

Early church writers such as Irenaeus and Tertullian noted that this gospel was written by John, "the disciple whom Jesus loved" (John 13:23), and many details mentioned in the book seem to reflect the recollections of an eyewitness. John wrote this gospel to all people around AD 85 to proclaim Jesus as the Son of God who operated with his Father's full authority. The most unique of the gospel accounts, John's gospel goes the deepest theologically, touching on issues such as the incarnation (John 1) and the ministry of the Holy Spirit (John 14 – 16). Also look for Jesus' seven "I am" statements here: the bread of life; the light of the world; the gate for the sheep; the good shepherd; the resurrection and the life; the way, truth, and life; and the true vine.

Acts 1 – 8

Written by Luke, the book of Acts begins with the post-resurrection appearance of Jesus to his disciples and then fast-forwards to his dramatic ascension to heaven. The first eight chapters in Acts focus primarily on the work of Peter and the other disciples in the early church as it took root and began to expand in the region. Notable accounts include the coming of the Holy Spirit on the day of Pentecost (Acts 2), Peter and John's arrest (Acts 4), Stephen's arrest and execution (Acts 6 – 7), and Philip's ministry to the Ethiopian eunuch (Acts 8).

READING

Each day this week, read the passages of Scripture indicated below. If it is helpful, use this chart to help you record your reading progress. Establish a reading schedule that works best for you — and then stick with it. Try to make it a habit to pray before you begin reading each day, asking God to use his Word to instruct and guide you. If you find you are behind in your reading, set aside extra time this week to catch up.

Day	Passage	☑
1	Mark 1 – 2; 6; 8 – 10; 12; 14 – 16	☐
2	Luke 1 – 6; 10; 12; 15; 19	☐
3	Luke 21 – 24; John 1 – 6; 8	☐
4	John 10 – 11; 13 – 15; 17; 20 – 21	☐
5	Acts 1 – 8	☐

STUDY QUESTIONS

1. What are some of the highlights — knowledge gained, puzzling questions, moments of insight — you experienced during your reading this week?

2. What are some of the different kinds of miracles Jesus performed? What was the response of the people? What was the response of the Pharisees?

3. How did Jesus show that his authority came from God (see Mark 2:6 – 12)?

4. Jesus taught his disciples that he must suffer in order to accomplish salvation for the world. How did the disciples respond to Jesus' words about suffering (see Mark 8:31 – 33)?

5. What does Jesus teach about servant leadership (see Mark 10:41 – 45)? How was servant leadership essential to Jesus' fulfillment of his task on earth?

6. How did Jesus describe his purpose in Luke 5:27 – 32? How does his teaching in the parable of the lost son (see Luke 15:11 – 31) and his interaction with Zacchaeus (see Luke 19:1 – 10) reflect this purpose?

7. List the "I am" statements that Jesus makes in the book of John (see especially John 14:6). What do these statements reveal about Jesus and his relationship to the Father? How does John 1:1, 14 reflect this relationship?

8. Describe the effect the coming of the Holy Spirit had on Jesus' followers. How do you see the words of Acts 1:8 being manifested in their lives? How was this a fulfillment of Jesus' promise in John 14:15 – 29?

9. What attitude characterized the believers in the early church (see Acts 4)? What made followers of Christ such as Stephen willing to endure persecution for the sake of the gospel?

Use the space below to write down any key points or questions you want to bring to the next group meeting.

12

A Brief Survey of
Mark – Acts 8

"The Son of Man came to seek and to save the lost."

LUKE 19:10

WELCOME

Welcome to session 12 of *A Brief Survey of the Bible*. Take a few minutes to go around the group and invite everyone to answer the following questions:

- What questions do we ask in order to find out more about a person?
- What are the characteristics of a person who has genuine authority?

READING FOLLOW-UP

1. What challenges did you face in getting your reading done? What was the most effective thing you did to meet those challenges?

2. As you read the Bible this week, what particular thoughts and/or events stood out to you or surprised you? Why?

3. What questions came up during your reading for which you'd like to find answers?

WATCH THE VIDEO

Play the video teaching segment for session 12. As you watch, use the following outline to record any thoughts or concepts that stand out to you.

Notes

Mark presents the Messiah with a crown of thorns and as a suffering servant. Christ comes to suffer and pay for the sins of the world by giving his life.

In the gospel of Mark, Jesus is the mighty Messiah, the Son of God, who teaches with authority. He speaks for God, has authority over demons, heals the sick, and calls the disciples, who drop everything and follow him. Mark 10:45 is the key verse of this gospel: "The Son of Man did not come to be served, but to serve, and to give his life as a ransom for many."

In the gospel of Luke, Jesus is the Savior for lost people everywhere. In Luke 5:30 – 31, Jesus says that he came to call the sinner to repentance.

Like the father in the parable of the lost son, God is always ready to welcome his wayward children home. Luke 19:10 is the theme verse of Luke's gospel: "For the Son of Man came to seek and to save the lost."

In the gospel of John, Jesus is the divine Son who reveals the Father. Jesus was fully God, yet he came to earth to reveal who God was (see John 1:14).

A key verse in John's gospel is John 14:6, where Jesus says, "I am the way and the truth and the life. No one comes to the Father except through me."

Luke wrote the book of Acts, and in its pages he continues his theme of God's love for lost people. In Acts we see the unstoppable progress of the gospel from Jerusalem to the ends of the earth. The power of the Holy Spirit, which Jesus promises in Acts 1:8, is key to this progress.

The gospel progresses geographically but also ethnically. It breaks down barriers as it moves from people to people. God's message is for the whole world.

GROUP DISCUSSION

Take a few minutes with your group members to discuss what you just watched and explore these concepts in Scripture.

1. As you watched the video, which particular points stood out to you? Which aspect of the video most enhanced your understanding of what you read this past week?

2. What do Jesus' words in Mark 10:45 mean to you? What was Jesus' purpose in serving others? Why was it necessary for him to become a "ransom" for us?

3. Why is it important to understand the suffering that Jesus experienced on our behalf? What does his suffering say about his sacrifice? How does Jesus' attitude toward his suffering encourage us when life gets hard? What does it say about the cost of discipleship?

4. What does it mean to be self-righteous? What does it mean to acknowledge that we are sinners in need of a Savior? What is the difference between these two attitudes?

5. How, according to the Gospels, did Jesus seek the lost? In what ways have you experienced being "found" by Jesus?

6. Which of Jesus' "I am" statements in John's gospel means the most to you? What do they tell you about Jesus' desire for you?

7. Now that you have read all four Gospels, think about the portraits of Jesus they present. How does each picture help you get to know Jesus better? What new aspects did you discover about who Jesus is?

   Matthew: Jesus as the King of the Jews

   Mark: Jesus as a suffering servant

   Luke: Jesus as the Savior for lost people everywhere

   John: Jesus as the Son of God

8. The dwelling of the Holy Spirit in believers represents God's presence in the world. How does the Holy Spirit help believers spread the message of Christ? How has the Holy Spirit brought about change in your life? In what ways are you participating in Jesus' plan for spreading the gospel that is given in Acts 1:8?

LIVING THE WORD

For this activity, each group member will need a map of your country (free maps can be downloaded online and printed), a compass, and a pen.

Read Acts 1:7 – 8 aloud in your small group, and then use the compass to draw a circle around your city of residence on the map. Label this circle "Jerusalem." Draw a larger circle around that one to incorporate several states, any nearby countries, and/or islands outside your city's geography. Label that area "Samaria." Outside that circle, label the area "the ends of the earth." Now list the people you have served in the name of the gospel in each area — your "Jerusalem," "Samaria," and "ends of the earth." Close your time in prayer, and as you pray, add any names to the map that come to mind where you have an opportunity to be a witness.

CLOSING PRAYER

Use the following prayer to close out your group time, or feel free to say one of your own.

> *Lord, we are humbled that you choose to be present in our lives. Thank you for the presence, strength, and guidance of the Holy Spirit for all who call you Lord and Savior. We know you want your presence to be spread to the rest of the world, and we thank you for making us instruments in that plan. We know you will provide us with boldness, words, and opportunities as we follow your guidance and serve as your witnesses. We offer ourselves for your glory. Amen.*

Did You Know?

- When John the Baptist called Jesus "the Lamb of God," he used a phrase that was related to the Old Testament sacrifices (see Leviticus 4:32 – 35; Isaiah 53:4 – 12). Just as in Old Testament times when an animal could be sacrificed as an atonement for the sin that separated a person from the holy God (see Leviticus 17:11), Jesus came to earth as God's "Lamb" to shed his blood for the removal of the sins of the entire world. (*Zondervan Handbook to the Bible*)

- The city of Jerusalem during Jesus' time was much larger than it had been during the days of King David. The wealthier people lived in a newer upper city section west of the former City of David. The temple bordered the northern boundary of David's former city and overlooked the Mount of Olives and the garden of Gethsemane to the east. It accounted for about a fifth of the city. Herod's palace was in the upper western corner of the Upper City. Golgotha, the traditional site of Jesus' crucifixion, was just north of Herod's palace outside the city wall. (*Zondervan Handbook to the Bible*)

- When Jesus taught, he often used images that were familiar to his audience. For example, while in Jerusalem during the Feast of Shelters, he identified himself as "the light of the world." This was meaningful because at dusk the feast participants held a ceremony in which they lit four golden candelabra. These symbolized the pillar of fire that God had used during the exodus to guide his people through the desert wilderness at night.

- One way to gain a picture of God's entire story in the Bible is to think of it this way: (1) the Old Testament is a record of God the Father; (2) the Gospels are a record of God the Son; and (3) the books of Acts through Revelation are a record of God the Spirit.

On Your Own
Between-Sessions Personal Study

This week, you explored God's story in the books from Mark – Acts 8. In the next session, you will be discussing key stories and principles from the remainder of Acts through the book of Philemon. Use the following between-sessions material to give you some background on these books and guide your reading for the week.

OVERVIEW

The following is a brief overview of the books you and your group will cover during next week's session. Take a moment to review this information, and at the end of the section note any questions you want to discuss with your group.

Acts 9 – 28

In Acts 7 we are introduced to a new character who will come to occupy the majority of the remaining chapters in Acts. This young man is named Saul, but after he meets the risen Jesus on the road to Damascus, his name will be changed to Paul. Luke goes on to relate the events of Paul's three missionary journeys as he takes the gospel "to the ends of the earth" (Acts 13:4 – 14:28; 15:39 – 18:22; 18:23 – 21:17), and also his journey to Rome (Acts 27:1 – 28:16). As you read, notice the powerful work of the Holy Spirit in the lives of Christ's followers as they fulfill Christ's command to be his witnesses.

Romans

The remainder of the New Testament is primarily made up of letters, or epistles, written by Paul, James, Peter, John, and Jude. The books of Romans – 2 Thessalonians are letters from Paul to specific churches, most of which he founded during his missionary journeys. Paul likely wrote Romans in AD 57 to the church in Rome (which he did not found) to provide an overview of his theology, and it is widely regarded as his greatest letter. As you read his words, pay attention to how often he emphasizes the fundamentals of Christian belief — especially that faith in Christ's death and resurrection is the only ground for salvation by God.

1 Corinthians

Paul wrote this letter to the church in Corinth, a thriving city in Greece, around AD 55 in response to information he received about divisions and deteriorating spiritual conditions in the church. The theme of the letter revolves around these problems and stresses the need for believers in Christ to continually develop holy character.

2 Corinthians

After writing 1 Corinthians, Paul apparently made a "painful visit" to the church in Corinth and wrote a "severe letter" (now lost) to correct the abuses he found. When he heard that letter had achieved its desired effect, he drafted this letter to express his joy, explain the troubles he had experienced for the gospel, and educate them on living the Christian life. Paul wrote the letter in two stages, as in 2 Corinthians 10 – 13 he refutes false teachers who had come to challenge his authority as an apostle. Paul emphasizes the integrity he modeled in their midst, warns them to deal with the troublemakers, and tells them to prepare for his next visit.

Galatians

Paul wrote this letter sometime around AD 48 to churches in the province of Galatia that he had helped to found. The occasion was the appearance of false teachers who were telling believers that in order to follow Christ they also had to become Jews. Paul pointed out the familiar trap into which these religious Jews had fallen — the temptation to teach that works, and not grace alone, was necessary to receive God's salvation.

Ephesians

Paul likely wrote this letter in AD 60 to believers in the church at Ephesus and in western Asia Minor. Paul had made Ephesus his base of operations for more than two years, during which he had proclaimed the gospel throughout the region (see Acts 19:10). Unlike his other letters, Paul does not address any particular errors or heresies in the church. Rather, he seeks to help believers better understand God's purpose and grace to them and to appreciate the high goals God has established for the church. Paul notes in Ephesians 3:1 that he is "a prisoner of Christ," and this imprisonment most likely occurred when he was placed under house arrest in Rome (see Acts 28:16 – 31). For this reason, Ephesians, Philippians, Colossians, and Philemon are known as the "prison epistles."

Philippians

Paul wrote this letter to the church in Philippi, a prosperous Roman colony, sometime around AD 61 to encourage the believers to be unified and not allow divisions to come between them. He also exhorted them to stand firm in the face of persecution and rejoice regardless of their circumstances. Philippians is Paul's most joyful epistle, and he uses the word *joy* (in its various Greek forms) some sixteen times in the letter.

Colossians

Paul wrote this letter to the church in Colossae, a former leading city in Asia Minor, sometime around AD 60. Paul's purpose appears to be to refute some false teachings and heresies that had taken hold in the community. The heresies are diverse in nature and seem to be a mixture of extreme forms of Judaism and Gnosticism — reliance on human wisdom and tradition. Paul refutes them by exalting the fullness of Christ as contrasted with the emptiness of philosophy.

1 Thessalonians

Paul and Silas founded the church in Thessalonica, a bustling seaport city in Macedonia, during their second missionary journey (see Acts 17:1 – 10). After having to leave the city abruptly, he penned this letter to them around AD 51 to encourage the believers who were now facing trials for their faith. He praises them for their perseverance, instructs them in godly living, and answers questions they have about the return of Christ.

2 Thessalonians

Paul's purpose in writing this letter, which he penned in AD 51 or 52, was to again encourage the believers and correct misunderstandings that had arisen concerning Jesus' return. He also urges the believers to be steadfast and work for a living.

1 Timothy

Paul wrote this letter to Timothy, his younger assistant who had been overseeing the church in Ephesus, sometime around AD 64. This letter, 2 Timothy, and Titus are known as the "pastoral epistles," or letters from Paul to encourage his two close coworkers in their ministry. In this letter Paul gives Timothy instructions for supervising the church, refutes false teachings, and guides Timothy in dealing with different groups of people in the congregation.

2 Timothy

After Paul's release from prison in Rome in AD 62, he was again imprisoned in AD 66. This time he was placed in a dungeon and put in chains like a common criminal. Paul knew his life was nearing an end, so he wrote this final letter to charge Timothy to guard the gospel, persevere in the face of the mounting persecution, and keep on spreading the good news of Christ.

Titus

Paul wrote this letter to Titus, a Gentile convert who was a trusted partner in ministry, sometime around AD 63 – 65. He had left Titus on the island of Crete to organize the new church and complete some needed work there. In this letter, he gives Titus guidance on how to meet opposition, instruct the community in faith and conduct, and combat false teachings.

Philemon

Paul wrote this letter to a believer named Philemon in Colossae sometime around AD 60. Philemon was a slave owner, and one of those slaves (named Onesimus) had stolen from him, escaped, and then become a Christian. This was an offense deserving of death under Roman law, but in this letter Paul appeals to Philemon to accept Onesimus as a Christian brother.

READING

Each day this week, read the passages of Scripture indicated below. If it is helpful, use this chart to help you record your reading progress. Establish a reading schedule that works best for you — and then stick with it. Try to make it a habit to pray before you begin reading each day, asking God to use his Word to instruct and guide you. If you find you are behind in your reading, set aside extra time this week to catch up.

Day	Passage	☑
1	Acts 9 – 13; 15; 21 – 22; 27 – 28; Romans 1; 3	☐
2	Romans 6 – 10; 12; 15; 1 Corinthians 1; 5; 9; 13	☐
3	2 Corinthians 1; 5 – 6; 10 – 12; Galatians 1 – 3; 5; Ephesians 2; 4; 6	☐
4	Philippians 2 – 4; Colossians 1 – 3; 1 Thessalonians 1 – 2; 4 – 5; 2 Thessalonians 1 – 3	☐
5	1 Timothy 1 – 2; 4; 6; 2 Timothy 2 – 4; Titus 1 – 3; Philemon	☐

STUDY QUESTIONS

1. What are some of the highlights — knowledge gained, puzzling questions, moments of insight — you experienced during your reading this week?

2. Looking at Paul's upbringing, how was he uniquely qualified to address many of the issues faced by the early church (see Acts 21)? What were some of these issues?

3. What did Paul say was essential for salvation (see Romans 10:13 and Ephesians 2:8 – 9)? What was happening in many of the churches Paul had helped found that was leading believers away from these basic truths (or adding to them)?

4. What was the threat that false teachers posed to the early church? How did Paul say their messages took away from Jesus' sacrifice on the cross (see Colossians 1:15 – 23 and 2:6 – 9)?

5. How did Paul describe the freedom the gospel brings? How does this freedom change the hearts of those who believe in Jesus (see Galatians 3:23 – 29)?

6. Paul told the Christians in Thessalonica to keep striving — even beyond the faith-fulness they had already displayed (see 1 Thessalonians 4:1 – 2). What does this admonition say about investing in the Christian life after conversion?

7. Paul directed Timothy and Titus to make disciples — to pass the message of the gospel on to others and equip them to do the same. Why was this an urgent priority for Paul?

8. What did you learn about the elements of healthy spiritual growth in the church body? What factors contributed to helping the early Christians grow together in love and Christlikeness (see Philippians 2:1 – 5)?

Use the space below to write down any key points or questions you want to bring to the next group meeting.

13

A Brief Survey of
Acts 9 – Philemon

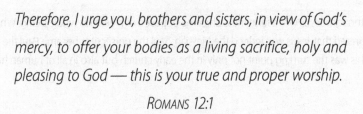

Therefore, I urge you, brothers and sisters, in view of God's
mercy, to offer your bodies as a living sacrifice, holy and
pleasing to God — this is your true and proper worship.

ROMANS 12:1

WELCOME

Welcome to session 13 of *A Brief Survey of the Bible*. Take a few minutes to go around the group and invite everyone to answer the following questions:

- What does it mean to mentor someone?
- What are the characteristics of an effective mentor?

READING FOLLOW-UP

1. What challenges did you face in getting your reading done? What was the most effective thing you did to meet those challenges?

2. As you read the Bible this week, what particular thoughts and/or events stood out to you or surprised you? Why?

3. What questions came up during your reading for which you'd like to find answers?

WATCH THE VIDEO

Play the video teaching segment for session 13. As you watch, use the following outline to record any thoughts or concepts that stand out to you.

Notes

Saul thought Jesus was a false messiah, so he opposed him with his whole being. When he recognized that Jesus was indeed the Messiah, Saul the persecutor became Paul the apostle. This was the turning point not only in the early church but also in all of human history.

The word *apostle* means a messenger, or one sent out with a commission. Paul took his commission seriously — to take the gospel to the whole world.

We read the letters of Paul like any other kind of letters. We ask questions such as, "To whom were they written?" "Why were they written?" "Who wrote them?"

Romans is widely viewed as Paul's greatest letter. In it, Paul gives the Romans an overview of his theology so they can become partners in his ministry to spread the gospel.

Romans 12 shows us how we are to live in response to salvation. Paul talks about being a living sacrifice and offering ourselves to God. This is a whole new level of sacrifice.

Paul wrote each of his letters to address a specific concern. Galatians addressed false teachers; Thessalonians encouraged the church as it faced persecution and trials; Philippians addressed unity in the church; and Timothy addressed making disciples and leading the church.

Paul believed the way to reach the world was by making disciples, and he passed that vision on to Timothy and Titus. This is also the message for us to pass on to others.

GROUP DISCUSSION

Take a few minutes with your group members to discuss what you just watched and explore these concepts in Scripture.

1. As you watched the video, which particular points stood out to you? Which aspect of the video most enhanced your understanding of what you read this past week?

2. How would you describe Paul's commitment to his mission to take the gospel to the whole world? How did he demonstrate this fervor? What motivated him? How has Paul's example influenced your sense of mission to share Jesus with others?

3. Which accounts of the experiences of the early Christians do you find most remarkable? What struggles did they have that would be the most difficult for you to handle?

4. In Romans 12, Paul talks about being living sacrifices. How has your salvation experience affected your daily life? What changes occurred? Where do you need to stimulate growth and risk being a sacrifice for Christ?

5. In 2 Timothy 3:16 – 17, Paul tells us why it is important for us to read and study the Bible. In what ways has reading the Bible proven to be useful and made you better equipped for every good work? How has reading the Bible protected you from wrong thinking or actions?

6. Which of Paul's instructions on godly living hits the closest to home for you? Why? In what ways do you need God's help and the encouragement of other believers to make changes or renew your commitment in this area?

7. What does unity in the church look like? How is unity different from compromise?

8. What would you identify as the key themes of this portion of Scripture? What impact can what you've just seen make on your life today?

LIVING THE WORD

For this activity, everyone will need paper and a pen.

In your small group, take a few moments to write down the difference God's salvation through Jesus has made in your life. This is not a time of confession, so you don't have to include specific personal details — just focus on what God has done to bring growth. If you are comfortable in doing so, share your testimony of being made new in Christ with your group. While this may not be easy for you, if you are willing to take the risk you will reap the benefits of seeing how your story can inspire another person. Hearing each other's stories can encourage your faith and spur you on to continued growth.

CLOSING PRAYER

Use the following prayer to close out your group time, or feel free to say one of your own.

> *Thank you, Lord Jesus, that we can be part of spreading your good news of salvation. As we study your Word and seek your wisdom in our lives, empower us with your Holy Spirit to be living sacrifices, ready to serve you. We ask for your strength to continue to grow in our faith and share it with others. Amen.*

Did You Know?

- The early Christians believed the long-awaited coming of Jesus fulfilled ancient Old Testament prophecies concerning the Messiah, and they viewed themselves as participants in the ongoing story of God's dealings with humankind. Jesus — God in human form — had come to earth personally to rescue all of humanity from sinful rebellion. No wonder these Christians studied the Old Testament diligently! No wonder they joyously proclaimed him and his message to people everywhere so the news spread throughout the world! No wonder they rejoiced in the eternal life they would one day receive!

- In Acts 17:5 – 8, we read that angry Jews in Thessalonica dragged Christians before the city officials. In this instance, the Greek word translated "city ruler," *politarch*, has not been found anywhere else in Greek literature. However, in 1835 this word was discovered on an ancient arch that spanned the Egnatian Way on the west side of Thessalonica. In 1867 the arch was destroyed, but the block containing the inscription is now in the British Museum in London. (*NIV Study Bible*, note for Acts 17:6)

- New Christians in the Greek city of Corinth faced great temptations and challenges as they learned to follow Christ. At least twelve pagan temples were located there, including one dedicated to Aphrodite, the goddess of love and sex. According to the Greek geographer Strabo (63 BC – AD 24), followers of Aphrodite worshiped her by practicing religious prostitution with as many as 1,000 sacred priestesses. Immorality in Corinth became so rampant that the Greek verb translated "to Corinthianize" came to mean "to practice sexual immorality." (*NIV Study Bible*, notes for 1 Corinthians 6:18; 7:2)

- In Paul's letters, he often refers to the disciple Peter as Cephas, which apparently was an Aramaic form of the name Peter (see Galatians 2:7 – 14), and to Silas as Silvanus, which appears to be a Roman rendering of the Greek name Silas. Other companions he mentions include Barnabas, James, John, Timothy, Aquila, Apollos, and Jason, all of whom appear in the book of Acts. However, one name that is remarkably absent from Acts is Titus, Paul's trusted coworker in his ministry, whom he names many times in his epistles. Various theories have been put forward as to why Luke omitted his name (including the possibility that he was the Titius Justus mentioned in Acts 18:7), but ultimately the reason is unknown.

On Your Own
Between-Sessions
Personal Study

This week, you explored God's story from Acts 9 through Paul's letter to Philemon. In the next session, you will be discussing key stories and principles from Hebrews – Revelation, the final books in the Bible. Use the following between-sessions material to give you some background on these books and guide your reading for the week.

OVERVIEW

The following is a brief overview of the books you and your group will cover during next week's session. Take a moment to review this information, and at the end of the section note any questions you want to discuss with your group.

Hebrews

The author of this letter is anonymous, and even the early church fathers were uncertain who had written it (though many ascribed it to Paul). Based on the personal comments, it is clear the writer was well known to the recipients, and the fact he was well versed in the Old Testament has led many to believe he was either Barnabas or Apollos, a Jewish Christian known to have notable intellectual and oratorical abilities. The letter was likely penned from AD 67 – 70. As you read Hebrews, which some view as a condensation of the entire Bible, pay close attention to the themes relating to Jesus' identity and accomplishments. Note his position as our "great high priest," the new covenant he established, and the call to follow him faithfully. Also carefully observe the many Old Testament references the writer employs.

James

The author of this letter identifies himself as James, whom most believe was the brother of Jesus and leader of the Jerusalem council (see Acts 15). Interestingly, at first James did not believe Jesus was the Messiah and even challenged him (see John 7:2 – 5). However, after Jesus appeared to him (see 1 Corinthians 15:7), he became a pillar of the church. James's central theme is the need for believers to put their faith into action through good works. He also includes instruction on resisting temptation, maintaining faith, taming the tongue, and dealing with worldliness and oppression. James might have been written as early as AD 50.

1 Peter

The author of both 1 and 2 Peter identifies himself as the apostle Peter. Assuming this is true, the letters would have been written around AD 60 – 64 — after Paul's prison letters (with which the author shows familiarity) but before Peter's death in AD 67 or 68. The main theme of the letter is an exhortation for believers to stand firm in the face of suffering and persecution. As you read, look for what God reveals to you about living wholeheartedly for him, particularly in the areas of personal holiness, submission to authority, and humility. Consider, too, Peter's warnings about false teachers and being prepared for the second coming of Christ.

2 Peter

In Peter's second letter, he gives advice on how believers can deal with the rise of false teachers and evildoers who were appearing in the church. He also encourages believers to grow in Christ, reject false teaching, and watch for the Lord's return. Because 2 Peter and Jude are very similar, it is believed one borrowed from the other or that they drew from a common source.

1, 2, 3 John

Church tradition held that John, the beloved disciple and author of the gospel that bears his name, was not martyred but lived to an advanced age. The letters he wrote are difficult to date, but evidence suggests a date from AD 85 – 95. In John's first letter, he writes to assure believers of the certainty of their salvation and to refute heretical teachings that Jesus was not fully human and fully divine. The letters of 2 and 3 John are more personal in nature and respectively addressed to "the lady chosen by God" and "my dear friend Gaius." Within them, John encourages Christians to walk in love and show hospitality to those who bring Jesus' teaching and proclaim the truth.

Jude

Most believe Jude (Greek Judas) was another brother of Christ (see Matthew 13:55). In this short book, Jude encourages believers everywhere to persevere in faith and guard against false teachers in the church. These false teachers were perverting the gospel by saying that grace meant the freedom to sin. Jude could have been written as early as AD 65 and as late as AD 80.

Revelation

The early church fathers held that this book was written by the disciple John, though others from the third century on suggested the author was John the Elder. The letter was likely written at the time Christians were suffering persecution under the Roman emperor Domitian in AD 95. The book is typically difficult for modern readers because it was written in a form of literature known as apocalyptic, which is highly symbolic, and also combines elements common to epistles and prophetic literature. One item that is clear is that the book looks forward to the triumph to come at the return of Christ, when he will deliver the righteous who are suffering and judge the wicked for their deeds. Notice the author's call for believers to remain true to what they were taught regardless of what the world says to the contrary.

READING

Each day this week, read the passages of Scripture indicated below. If it is helpful, use this chart to help you record your reading progress. Establish a reading schedule that works best for you — and then stick with it. Try to make it a habit to pray before you begin reading each day, asking God to use his Word to instruct and guide you. If you find you are behind in your reading, set aside extra time this week to catch up.

Day	Passage	☑
1	Hebrews 1; 3; 8; 10 – 12; James 1 – 3	☐
2	James 4 – 5; 1 Peter 1 – 5; 2 Peter 1 – 3	☐
3	1 John 1 – 5; 2 John; 3 John; Jude	☐
4	Revelation 1 – 8; 11 – 13	☐
5	Revelation 14 – 22	☐

STUDY QUESTIONS

1. What are some of the highlights — knowledge gained, puzzling questions, moments of insight — you experienced during your reading this week?

2. How does the author of Hebrews encourage his Jewish readers to look forward? How does he warn them against looking to the past (see Hebrews 1:1 – 3)? What position or status does he describe for Jesus (see Hebrews 1:3 – 4 and 3:1 – 6)?

3. How is Jesus' sacrifice on the cross different from the sacrifices made in the Old Testament by the high priest at the temple (see Hebrews 10:1 – 14)? How do the words *new* and *better* describe what Christ has done?

4. What does James say is the difference between *claiming* to be a Christian and actually *possessing* an authentic faith (see James 1:22 and 2:14)? According to James, what effect will true faith have on a person's life?

5. What reason does Peter give for the suffering that Christians were experiencing (see 1 Peter 4:12 – 19)? How is this perspective on suffering different from the world's view of suffering?

6. Second Peter, 1 and 2 John, and Jude all address the problem of false teachers in the believers' midst. What is the fate of those who teach false doctrine (see 2 Peter 2)? What does the recurrence of this theme tell us about the importance of having sound doctrine?

7. What is the Christian's response to God's love (see 1 John 4:7 – 5:5)? What words of encouragement do you find in this passage? What assurance of salvation does John describe for believers (see 1 John 4:13)?

8. A key theme in Revelation is God's sovereignty over human history (see Revelation 22:7, 12 – 13). How does John say this should affect the faith of those who belong to Christ (see Revelation 2:7, 11, 17, 27 – 29; 3:5 – 6, 13, 21)? How would John's pictures of heaven and Jesus' return have instilled hope and strength in believers and helped them to persevere?

9. What emotions do the passages you have read in Revelation stir up in you? How do you view the events John describes? What hope does John's vision of the new heaven and new earth in Revelation 22 provide to you?

Use the space below to write down any key points or questions you want to bring to the next group meeting.

14

A Brief Survey of
Hebrews – Revelation

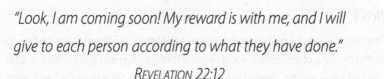

"Look, I am coming soon! My reward is with me, and I will

give to each person according to what they have done."

REVELATION 22:12

WELCOME

Welcome to the final session of *A Brief Survey of the Bible*! Take a few minutes to go around the group and invite everyone to answer the following questions:

- How do people generally respond to suffering and persecution?
- How is suffering for your faith different from other kinds of persecution?

READING FOLLOW-UP

1. What challenges did you face in getting your reading done? What was the most effective thing you did to meet those challenges?

2. As you read the Bible this week, what particular thoughts and/or events stood out to you or surprised you? Why?

3. What questions came up during your reading for which you'd like to find answers?

WATCH THE VIDEO

Play the video teaching segment for session 14. As you watch, use the following outline to record any thoughts or concepts that stand out to you.

Notes

The first four books of the general epistles (Hebrews – 2 Peter) focus on how to stand fast in the face of persecution and *external* threats. The next five epistles (1 John – Revelation) focus on the *internal* threat that comes from false teaching, and point to the true gospel.

The book of Hebrews was written to a group of Jewish Christians who were in danger of reverting back to Judaism. The writer reminds them that Jesus offers a better revelation, a better priesthood, a better sacrifice for sin, and a better covenant.

Today we have the Holy Spirit living in us, writing God's law on our hearts. The new covenant says everyone can know God directly without a mediator.

James says that anyone can profess to have faith in Jesus, but that doesn't make a person a Christian. True faith in Jesus Christ is what makes a person a Christian; this naturally results in a life transformed from the inside out.

Peter tells Christians in his first epistle that those who believe in Jesus *will* suffer. They will suffer because they are aliens in this world — their true home is with God. For this reason, believers in Christ should not be surprised by persecution.

In Revelation 2:9, we find that John was suffering on Patmos when he saw a vision of what God had in store for the world. God started human history, and he will bring it to its ultimate conclusion. Jesus is the Alpha and the Omega, the Beginning and the End.

Jesus is the agent of God's salvation; he is the climax of the story. Jesus holds the keys to death, which is humanity's greatest fear. We can have life because of who Jesus is.

Because God is sovereignly in control of human history, we can stay faithful and trust him. We are blessed if we read God's Word, hear it, and take it to heart (see Revelation 1:3). Christ could come at any time, so we need to use our time to bring him glory and take his message of salvation to the ends of the earth.

GROUP DISCUSSION

Take a few minutes with your group members to discuss what you just watched and explore these concepts in Scripture.

1. As you watched the video, which particular points stood out to you? Which aspect of the video most enhanced your understanding of what you read this past week?

2. Running a race means you are always focused forward. How does this perspective help you move on from past failures and unhealthy religious beliefs? How does it help you persevere in the midst of difficulties? How do those faithful witnesses who have gone before and are cheering you on encourage you to race well (see Hebrews 12:1)?

3. How does the author of Hebrews say Jesus' sacrifice was perfect? How does the adequacy of what Jesus did for you show up in your daily life? In how you view yourself? What evidence is there in your life that your faith in Christ is authentic?

4. How do false teachings creep into the church even today? What is your defense against falling prey to them? How can you strengthen your stand against those beliefs that try to pull you away from Christ?

5. What impact can suffering have on a person's faith? How does sharing your suffering with those in the body of Christ affect your faith? What does suffering for your faith look like in your situation? How is this different from suffering for other reasons?

6. How does confidence in God's sovereignty over human history give you the ability to face whatever happens in this world without fear? How does it help you respond when things happen on this earth that don't make sense to you?

7. How has your picture of Jesus as the Savior expanded through your study of these Scriptures? What misconceptions have you needed to get past?

8. How does the perspective that Jesus is coming back influence your outlook on life? What are you doing in your everyday life to remain watchful for his return?

LIVING THE WORD

For this activity, group members will need a pen and the description of their relationship with God that they created in session 1. (Those participants not present for session 1 will need a blank piece of paper and an envelope to complete the exercise.)

To conclude your time together, review the description of your relationship with God that you wrote at the beginning of this study. How have you seen your relationship change and grow? What challenges to your faith have you encountered? How did you respond? On your paper, write a new description of your relationship with God, identifying areas of spiritual growth, questions you may have, and changes you would like to see in the future. Make a commitment to return to this description in the upcoming month and add a new description based on your current walk of faith with Christ.

CLOSING PRAYER

As a way of wrapping up the study, you and your group will take part in a responsive reading from selected verses in Revelation 21 – 22. This passage serves as a reminder of the eternity that awaits followers of Jesus Christ and provides a beautiful benediction to your overall group experience.

Facilitator: Then I saw "a new heaven and a new earth," for the first heaven and the first earth had passed away, and there was no longer any sea. I saw the Holy City, the new Jerusalem, coming down out of heaven from God, prepared as a bride beautifully dressed for her husband. And I heard a loud voice from the throne saying, "Look! God's dwelling place is now among the people, and he will dwell with them. They will be his people, and God himself will be with them and be their God. He will wipe every tear from their eyes. There will be no more death or mourning or crying or pain, for the old order of things has passed away." (21:1 – 4)

Group: Thank you, Lord, for your desire to live with us. Thank you for your faithfulness to us despite our unfaithfulness. Thank you for all you have done over thousands of years to make life with you possible.

Facilitator: He who was seated on the throne said, "I am making everything new!" Then he said, "Write this down, for these words are trustworthy and true." He said to me: "It is done. I am the Alpha and the Omega, the Beginning and the End. To the thirsty I will give water without cost from the spring of the water of life. Those who are victorious will inherit all this, and I will be their God and they will be my children. But the cowardly, the unbelieving, the vile, the murderers, the sexually immoral, those who practice magic arts, the idolaters and all liars — they will be consigned to the fiery lake of burning sulfur. This is the second death." (21:5 – 8)

Group: Praise you, Lord, for your eternal presence. Praise you for making all things new. Thank you for sharing with us the cup of eternal life.

Facilitator: I, John, am the one who heard and saw these things. And when I had heard and seen them, I fell down to worship at the feet of the angel who had been showing them to me. But he said to me, "Don't do that! I am a fellow servant with you and with your fellow prophets and with all who keep the words of this scroll. Worship God!" Then he told me, "Do not seal up the words of the prophecy of this scroll, because the time is near." (22:8 – 10)

Group: Praise you, Lord, for your words of truth. We worship you.

Facilitator: "Look, I am coming soon! My reward is with me, and I will give to each person according to what they have done. I am the Alpha and the Omega, the First and the Last, the Beginning and the End.

"Blessed are those who wash their robes, that they may have the right to the tree of life and may go through the gates into the city. Outside are the dogs, those who practice magic arts, the sexually immoral, the murderers, the idolaters and everyone who loves and practices falsehood.

"I, Jesus, have sent my angel to give you this testimony for the churches. I am the Root and the Offspring of David, and the bright Morning Star."

The Spirit and the bride say, "Come!" And let the one who hears say, "Come!" Let the one who is thirsty come; and let the one who wishes take the free gift of the water of life. (22:12 – 17)

Group: Praise you, Lord, for sending Jesus, son of David, holy Lamb of God, to cleanse us from our sin.

Facilitator: I warn everyone who hears the words of the prophecy of this scroll: If anyone adds anything to them, God will add to that person the plagues described in this scroll. And if anyone takes words away from this scroll of prophecy, God will take away from that person any share in the tree of life and in the Holy City, which are described in this scroll. He who testifies to these things says, "Yes, I am coming soon." Amen. Come, Lord Jesus. The grace of the Lord Jesus be with God's people. Amen. (22:18 – 21)

Group: Bless your name, Lord Jesus! We wait for you.

Did You Know?

- During New Testament times, it is likely that more Jews lived in other countries than in their homeland. (An estimated one million lived in Egypt, for example.) Political tensions between the Romans and the Jews intensified after Jesus' death and resurrection. The Jews made their last stand against the Romans during the Jewish War in AD 66 – 73, during which time the Romans destroyed the temple. The remaining Jews scattered to other countries where, in colonies in various cities, they maintained their distinctive culture and lifestyle. In his travels, the apostle Paul made a point of visiting these expatriate Jewish communities to share the transforming message of Jesus. (*Zondervan Handbook to the Bible*)

- Up until the time of the Jewish War, the Jewish people lived in relative harmony with their Roman rulers. Julius Caesar and Augustus both supported laws that allowed Jews to worship as they chose. Although the emperor Claudius expelled the Jews from Rome in AD 19, they were soon allowed to return and resume their independent existence. The Romans viewed Christianity as a sect of Judaism, so they granted these same rights to Christians. All this changed in AD 64 when the Great Fire of Rome destroyed most of the city. Rumors began to circulate that the emperor Nero had started the fire to clear the way for a new palace he wanted to build. To deflect the blame, he began to target and persecute Christians.

- Hebrews is commonly referred to as a letter, but it does not contain the elements of the other letters we find in the New Testament. The author does not identify himself, there is no greeting, and the work overall is structured more like a sermon or essay. In addition, the eventual inclusion of the letter in the New Testament canon was not due to authorship (as with most of the other books) but because of its popularity and use among Christians. By the time the sixty-six books of the Bible that we know today were recognized in AD 397, the book of Hebrews had become widely accepted and viewed as inspired.

- The seven churches mentioned in Revelation 2–3 were located in places we can identify today. (1) Ephesus, an ancient city in the Roman province of Asia, is located near the town of Selcuk in Turkey, where its ruins can be found. (2) Smyrna, a small church, is in what is now named Izmir in western Turkey. (3) Pergamum, near the modern-day town of Bergama in western Turkey, was a center of emperor worship and had a huge altar dedicated to Zeus. (4) Thyatira, now the small town of Akhisar in western Turkey, was known for its purple dye. (5) Sardis, the capital of ancient Lydia, is about fifty miles east of Smyrna. (6) Philadelphia, about twenty-eight miles southeast of Sardis in present-day Turkey, was located near a broad and fertile valley. (7) Laodicea, now Latakia in Syria, was a prosperous banking center known for its eye salve and fine wool. The city, which had no water supply of its own, used lukewarm water channeled from hot springs in nearby Hierapolis. (*Zondervan Handbook to the Bible*)

Additional Resources for Group Facilitators

Thank you for your willingness to lead a group through *A Brief Survey of the Bible*. The rewards of being a leader are different from those of the individuals participating, and we hope you find your own walk with Jesus deepened by this experience. *A Brief Survey of the Bible* is a fourteen-session study built around video content and small group interaction. As group facilitator, your role will be to help your members explore God's Word and manage the behind-the-scenes details. To this end, there are several elements in this section that will help you effectively structure your time.

BEFORE YOU BEGIN

Before your first meeting, make sure group members have a copy of this study guide so they can follow along and write out their answers ahead of time. The guide will also provide suggested passages of Scripture for them to read throughout the week so they can be prepared for the next week's session. Give group members some time to look over the material and ask any preliminary questions. During your first meeting, be sure to send a sheet around the room and have the members write down their name, phone number, and email address so you can keep in touch with them during the week.

Generally, the ideal size for a group is between eight to ten people, which ensures everyone will have enough time to participate in discussions. If you have more people, you might want to break up the main group into smaller subgroups. Encourage those who show up at the first meeting to commit to attending for the duration of the study, as this will help the group members get to know each other, create stability for the group, and help you know how to prepare each week.

Note that each session begins with two "icebreaker" questions to get group members thinking about the topic for the week. Some people may want to tell a long story in response to one of these questions, but the goal is to keep the answers brief. Ideally, you want everyone in the group to get a chance to answer at least one of these opening questions, so try to keep the responses to a minute or less. If you have talkative group members, state up front that everyone needs to limit his or her answer to one minute.

Give group members a chance to answer, but tell them to feel free to pass if they wish. With the rest of the study, it's generally not a good idea to have everyone answer every question — a free-flowing discussion is more desirable. But with the opening icebreaker questions, you can go around the circle. Encourage shy people to share, but don't force them.

Before your first meeting, let group members know the bulk of their work will be done in between the main sessions, when they will read selected portions of Scripture over five days. Reading this material will enable them to see this study as a "survey" of the Bible and will prepare them for the video content they will view at the group meeting. During your group discussion time, participants will be drawing on the answers they wrote down, so encourage them to always complete these ahead of time. Also invite them to bring any questions and insights they uncovered while reading to your next meeting, especially if they had a breakthrough moment or if they didn't understand something.

WEEKLY PREPARATION

As the facilitator, there are a few things you should do to prepare for each meeting:

- *Read through the lesson.* This will help you become familiar with the content and know how to structure the discussion times.

- *Decide which questions you want to discuss.* Each session contains seven to nine discussion questions, so make sure you cover the questions that especially stood out to you.

- *Be familiar with the questions you want to discuss.* When the group meets, you'll be watching the clock, so you want to make sure you are familiar with the Bible study questions you have selected.

- *Read each session's "Living the Word" segment.* Several of these sections require materials you will need to provide at the meeting. Reading ahead will allow you to ask group members to bring items you need but don't have, and it will give you a sense of how to lead the group through the experience. Use the supply list in the next section to make sure you have what you need.

- *Pray for your group.* Pray for your group members throughout the week, and ask God to lead them as they study his Word.

- *Bring extra supplies to your meeting.* The members should bring their own pens for writing notes, but it's a good idea to have extras available for those who forget. You may also want to bring paper and additional Bibles.

Note that as you lead the discussion, in many cases there will be no one "right" answer to a question. Answers will vary, especially when the group members are being asked to share their personal experiences.

LIVING THE WORD SUPPLY LIST

Unless otherwise noted, make sure you have one of each of these items per participant.

Session 1: An Introduction

- Blank piece of paper
- Pen
- Envelope

Session 2: Genesis – Exodus

- A quarter
- Light-colored ¾-inch round labels (two per participant)
- Permanent marker

Session 3: Leviticus – Deuteronomy

- Copy of the Ten Commandments printed on card stock

Session 4: Joshua – 1 Samuel

- Pictures that represent the culture (provide as many as you can)
- Glue sticks
- Scissors
- Markers
- Large sheet of paper

Session 5: 2 Samuel – 2 Kings

- Blank notebook (participants can bring their own)
- Pen

Session 6: 1 Chronicles – Nehemiah

- Strip of card stock measuring 2" x 11"
- Pen

Session 7: Esther – Psalm 90

- Notecard
- Envelope

Session 8: Psalm 91 – Song of Songs

- Piece of paper measuring 11" x 17"
- Pen
- Bible
- Concordance (hard copy or electronic version)

Session 9: Isaiah – Lamentations

- Flower pot (six inches or larger)
- Permanent marker
- Small stones (several for each person)
- Water
- Potting soil
- Flower or vegetable seeds (several for each person)

Session 10: Ezekiel – Malachi

- Piece of paper
- Pencil

Session 11: Matthew

- Several worship songs (see description in session) and player
- Paper
- Pen

Session 12: Mark – Acts 8

- Map of your country
- Compass
- Pen

Session 13: Acts 9 – Philemon

- Paper
- Pen

Session 14: Hebrews – Revelation

- Paper and envelope the participants created in session 1, or blank piece of paper and envelope for those who did not complete that activity
- Pen

STRUCTURING THE DISCUSSION TIME

You will need to determine with your group how long you want to meet each week so you can plan your time accordingly. Generally, most groups like to meet for either sixty minutes or ninety minutes, so use one of the following schedules:

SECTION	60 MINUTES	90 MINUTES
Welcome (discuss the two opening questions)	5 minutes	10 minutes
Video (watch the video together as a group)	20 minutes	20 minutes
Group Discussion (discuss the Bible study questions)	20 minutes	40 minutes
Living the Word (do the closing activity)	10 minutes	10 minutes
Prayer (close in prayer)	5 minutes	10 minutes

As the group leader, it is up to you to keep track of the time and keep things moving along according to your schedule. You might want to set a timer for each segment so both you and the group members know when your time is up. (Note that there are some good phone apps for timers that play a gentle chime or other pleasant sound instead of a disruptive noise.)

Don't feel pressured to cover every question you have selected if the group has a good discussion going. Again, it's not necessary to go around the circle and make everyone share. Also don't be concerned if group members are quiet or slow to share. People are often quiet when they are pulling together their ideas, and this might be a new experience for them. Just ask a question and let it hang in the air until someone shares. You can then say, "Thank you. What about others? What came to you when you read through the passage?"

GROUP DYNAMICS

Leading a group through *A Brief Survey of the Bible* will prove to be highly rewarding both to you and your group. However, that doesn't mean you will not encounter any challenges along the way! Discussions can get off track. Group members may not be sensitive to the needs and ideas of others. Some might worry they will be expected to talk about matters that make them feel awkward. Others may express comments that result in disagreements. To help ease this strain on you and the group, consider the following ground rules:

- When someone raises a question or comment that is off the main topic, suggest dealing with it another time; or, if you feel led to go in that direction, let the group know you will be spending some time discussing it.

- If someone asks a question you don't know how to answer, admit it and move on. At your discretion, feel free to invite group members to comment on questions that call for personal experience.

- Respect group members' beliefs, whether they are new to the Bible or a lifetime student. It is not your responsibility to correct or even guide anyone's interpretation of what is being read. Rather, you want to encourage each person as he or she struggles with the Scripture's meaning.

- If you find that one or two people are dominating the discussion time, direct a few questions to others in the group. Outside the main group time, ask the more dominating members to help you draw out the quieter ones. Work to make them a part of the solution instead of the problem.

- When a disagreement occurs, encourage group members to process the matter in love. Encourage those on opposite sides to restate what they heard the other side say about the matter, and then invite each side to evaluate if that perception is accurate. Lead the group in examining other Scriptures related to the topic and look for common ground.

- Begin and end your small group sessions promptly. This will respect everyone's time and give the participants a framework in which to do the study.

When any issues arise, encourage your group members to follow the words from the Bible: "Love one another" (John 13:34); "If it is possible, as far as it depends on you, live at peace with everyone" (Romans 12:18); and "Be quick to listen, slow to speak and slow to become angry" (James 1:19).

CPSIA information can be obtained
at www.ICGtesting.com
Printed in the USA
LVHW040044221218
601418LV00006B/6/P